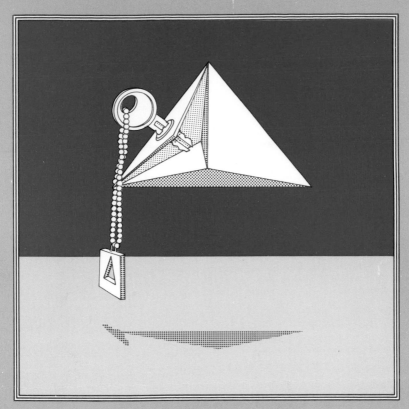

BUILDING CONTROLS INTO STRUCTURED SYSTEMS

▲

ALAN E. BRILL

▲

FOREWORD BY EDWARD YOURDON

BUILDING CONTROLS INTO STRUCTURED SYSTEMS

BUILDING CONTROLS INTO STRUCTURED SYSTEMS

ALAN E. BRILL

FOREWORD BY
EDWARD YOURDON

Yourdon Press
1133 Avenue of the Americas
New York, New York 10036

This book was set in Times Roman by YOURDON Press, 1133 Avenue of the Americas, New York, N.Y., using a PDP-11/70 running under the UNIX® operating system.*

---

*UNIX is a registered trademark of Bell Laboratories.

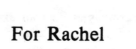

For Rachel

Acknowledgments

Creating a manuscript is at best an experience in terror. Having to put one's thoughts onto paper in cogent form is terrifying, but the unpleasantness can be mitigated — if you have the right people to work with. I'm lucky. I have.

First, there are my editors at Yourdon Press: Janice Wormington, Susan Moran, and Wendy Eakin. Without their encouragement and help, I would most certainly have been discouraged and helpless.

Second, my colleagues at YOURDON inc. provided the environment and the opportunity to prepare this book. In particular, I most sincerely appreciate the support of Ed Yourdon, Herb Morrow, and Tim Lister. I offer special thanks to Mike Fife, Debbie Gelman, and Carol Aarseth for keeping the administrative wolves from my door, and to George Armstrong for his artistry and his friendship.

Last, but first in my heart, I thank my wife, Linda, and my daughter, Rachel, for putting up with me during what I know were endless periods of elation and depression (depending on the state of the manuscript and the propensity of the computer on which I wrote it to work or not work). I love you both very much, and won't let it happen again (until the next book).

Contents

Preface

This is not a book about accounting. Nor, thankfully, is it a book about bookkeeping. In fact, it isn't primarily about auditing either. "What, then," you may ask, "is it about?" The answer is simple: It's about building *well-controlled* systems. How? By assuring that the systems contain what are called *internal accounting controls* of sufficient type and variety to provide *reasonable assurance* that the system is able to detect and handle any errors that are encountered.

"And why," you may also ask, "would I worry about internal accounting controls if not to placate the auditors?" Because internal control is a basic business requirement of *all* systems. True, auditors look at internal controls, but, believe it or not, they expect that you have built them into your systems because it is right to do so. Remember, the objective of most audits is not the detailed review of EDP controls, so there is often a very limited number of hours available to perform the EDP internal control review.

Consider a payroll system that has poor controls and doesn't detect that it occasionally adds $5,000 to a paycheck. Is this an auditing problem? Sure! The auditors will note it as evidence of ineffective control and will probably insist on independently verifying the work of the payroll system. But it's really *your* problem. How could you build a system that can't even detect such an obvious error?

Think about it: How many problems in your systems could have been prevented if you had more effective controls? Wouldn't the inevitable arrival of the auditors be less painful if you knew in advance that your systems were well controlled? The annual ritual of answering a scathing auditing report is without a doubt a painful and thankless job. Yet, we continue to build systems with poor controls and consequently set ourselves up for more aggravation.

Why you need this book

No matter how technically elegant or sophisticated they are, systems with poor internal controls are time bombs waiting to put your organization's credibility — and sometimes its very survival — at risk. The potential financial losses, bad publicity, embarrassment, and legal liability associated with ineffective controls just aren't worth the risk — particularly if you consider that it isn't difficult to put the right controls into a system when it's first built.

This book tells you how to build the right controls into your systems, how to document them, and how to painlessly inject consideration of internal controls into the entire systems development and quality assurance process.

As the title indicates, the focus of this book is on structured systems development, particularly systems development with structured analysis (DeMarco) and dataflow-based structured design (Yourdon-Constantine). At the heart of these techniques is the concept of developing a *model* of the system to be built; this model can be reviewed, modified, and repaired at a far lower cost than can the actual system.

The availability of a model is a key to success for the developer of system controls, since the control requirements of the model should match the control requirements of the final system. Using the model, the developer can check the proposed controls for completeness before the final system is built.

The benefits of well-controlled systems

Merely reading any book — including this one — won't markedly improve your systems development process; but if you apply the principles discussed in this book to your applications, you should expect

- far less aggravation when the auditors review your application systems

- a reduction in the application maintenance workload generated by modifications required by the internal and external auditors

- stabilized or in some cases reduced company auditing expenses (because well-controlled systems usually require less effort to audit than do poorly controlled systems)

- reduced risk of financial loss, bad publicity, embarrassment, and legal liability associated with failures of internal controls

- positive recognition by management of your businesslike approach to systems development

- fewer early morning calls when your system mysteriously de-synchronizes the general ledger master files

I recall a television commercial concerning the advantage of buying an oil filter costing only a few dollars to prevent hundreds of dollars of damage to your auto engine. It ends with a mechanic saying, "You can pay me now, or you can pay me later." The same is true with auditing. You *will* eventually have to put controls into your application systems. You can choose to wait until the auditors and your boss force you to do so, but wouldn't it be easier and more impressive if you took the initiative to *assure* that effective internal controls are a built-in part of every application system that you build?

Staten Island, New York   A.E.B.
May 1983

Foreword

I must admit that I first approached Al Brill's book with a great deal of trepidation. I've known Al for a few years now, and I wanted to like his book, but I wondered whether anyone could look forward to reading a book on accounting. Fortunately, Al removed all of my fears in the very first paragraph of the Preface, writing that it's not a book about accounting, or bookkeeping, or auditing. Whew!

And as it turned out, I had a delightful time reading the book. True to his word, Al didn't mention credits or debits even once, and he made the whole subject of building well-controlled systems pleasant and interesting.

In fact, there is much to learn from this book because auditing considerations and internal controls, as Al calls them, are foreign concepts to most programmers and systems analysts. Naturally, if you've worked on a payroll system or a general ledger system, such concepts may be obvious — but there are many, many people in the EDP profession who have not worked on systems so directly involved with money. That doesn't mean that these people don't have to know how to build controls into their systems. As Al points out, almost all business application programs manage information about *assets* of the corporation; indeed, the information itself is an asset, and information such as mailing lists and sales histories can be even more valuable than physical assets. In any case, whether the assets consist of manufactured products, or money, or information, they are valuable and deserve to be protected. Throughout the book, Al stresses a theme that I must agree with: Proper internal controls should be built into systems because it's *right* to do so, not just because of fear of a bad report from the outside auditing firm.

There are other themes running through the book that bring practical benefit. One theme near and dear to my heart deals with the relationship between internal controls and the concepts of structured analysis and structured design. Clearly, an auditor can't audit a system if he doesn't understand what the system is supposed to do, or if there's no documentation describing how the system carries out its goals. Those are the concerns of structured analysis and structured design, of course, and it is a pleasure to think that auditors will get just as much benefit from tools like data flow diagrams as the end-users of the system and the systems analysts.

Al has made an important contribution to the field by introducing the notion of phase-related controls. He observes that the structured techniques emphasize the difference between a model of the *requirements* of a system (which is built using structured analysis), and a model of the *implementation* of a system (which is built using structured design); he then suggests that auditing controls should be separated in the same way. Thus, some auditing controls should be considered part of the user policy and should be present regardless of the technology used to implement the system; other controls are design oriented and will vary considerably depending, for instance, on whether the system is implemented as a manual system, a batch system, or an on-line system. A simple idea — but one that I suspect will profoundly improve the process of designing controls into a system.

Al's book should be read carefully by members of the data processing profession and by members of the auditing profession — and also by the users who pay for computer systems to be built in the first place. Auditors need to learn more about the impact that structured analysis and structured design can have on their business; data processing people need to appreciate that internal controls are not something to be ignored or dismissed as intellectually trivial; and users need to appreciate that they can't just shrug their shoulders and assume that the systems they ask for will automatically have the proper controls built in.

New York, New York   Ed Yourdon
June 1983

BUILDING CONTROLS INTO STRUCTURED SYSTEMS

1 | Why Your Systems Must Be Controlled

The internal controls — those parts of the system that ensure the accuracy, completeness, and security of the system's data — aren't optional. They are absolute requirements. Consider the following statement: A system without effective internal controls is useless. Sound strong? It's meant to. In today's business and government organizations, virtually every asset is in some way managed, manipulated, or maintained by information systems. It stands to reason that those systems must, by definition, properly control those assets. If they can't control them properly, they are *bad* systems.

1.1 Systems that control and manage assets

Most systems manage and control valuable company assets. Hence, when a system is protected against error or sabotage, so are the assets it manipulates. Within the system, these assets take the form of data; sometimes the data itself is the asset. Most of the data that application systems manipulate can be placed into one of four categories:

- *Financial data:* data in accounts receivable and payable systems, for example; in billing systems; in payroll, general ledger, and cash management systems; and in many other systems that manipulate or report on financial assets.

- *Data about people:* information about people in personnel record-keeping and management systems, in staff assignment systems, and in so-called skill banks. This growing family of application systems helps organizations manage and utilize their human resources more

1

effectively. More and more, the importance of manag-. ing human resources well is being recognized, and the systems supporting this vital function are being improved.

- *Data on physical goods:* data in systems that affect or control assets (such as inventories of raw materials, finished goods, plant and equipment, real estate, or other physical entities, as well as order entry and fulfillment systems).

- *Information:* data in systems that don't fit into the financial, people, or goods categories.*

It could be said that the data processing department represents the greatest concentration of power in today's business and governmental organizations because the records stored and processed by the computers are, in large part, the total assets of the organization. Or, at the least, they are the *records* of assets that management uses for decision making purposes. Your bank, for example, doesn't maintain a strongbox in which your money is stored. Your account exists only as a magnetic pattern on the surface of a disk or tape.

1.2 Asset protection requires asset control

No one questions the need for effective control over cash, physical inventories, or check-signing machine signature plates, probably because it is easy to imagine the bad things that can happen to physical assets. The need for comprehensive but cost-effective controls on nonphysical assets should be as obvious as is the need for controls on physical assets, but it isn't.

1.2.1 How systems traditionally get controls

How do systems traditionally get controls? There are four ways: by chance, by user insistence, by auditor intervention, and by DP's recognition of the problem. As an auditor, I sometimes encounter sys-

---

*As an example of information-type data, Henry Luce III, vice president of Time, Inc., reported, in a 1980 speech before the Computer Security Institute, that his company reckoned its magazine and book subscriber file to have a value of $1.5 billion and its file of cable television subscribers to have another $1 billion in assets. Two files: $2.5 billion in assets. (As the late Senator Everett M. Dirksen said, "A billion dollars here, a billion dollars there, and pretty soon you're talking real money.")

tems that have pretty good controls even though not one of the systems developers ever thought about them. The controls somehow evolved purely by chance. Relying on chance is a poor way to develop controls in systems that are expected to control assets.

When users insist on controls, they can get them built into their systems, but users typically don't insist. Many users assume that the DP department is taking care of the controls. Others think that computers don't need the same kind of control that is necessary in non-computerized systems. The majority of users simply don't think about controls at all in their automated systems.

If you've got sufficient EDP auditors to analyze systems under development, they can review and specify controls. However, most companies don't have qualified auditors. In some informal surveys among the several hundred people attending seminars I've recently led, the ratio of DP people to EDP auditors ran hundreds to one. For the attendees from several big, well-known organizations, the ratio was more than a thousand to one. Imagine, if you will, that you are the one and only EDP auditor in a company with a DP staff of a thousand. How will you use your time efficiently? (Spending your time crying sounds realistic, but isn't hugely productive.) Specifically, how much time and attention can you give to recommending controls over applications? Not much! There just aren't enough EDP internal control professionals (and I'm including both auditors and quality assurance/quality control specialists) to give me (and, I hope, you) the feeling that I can rest easy. The resources necessary to give confidence just aren't there.

The experience of EDP auditors and quality assurance specialists alike is that application systems are often poorly controlled. But when the lack of control is brought to light, the data processing specialists, working with the users, *can* do a good job of adding controls. (Of course, it costs more and is more difficult to retrofit controls into a system that has already been designed than to build them in during the design process.) The problem, explored in detail in Chapter 5, is that systems developers generally don't think about building control and security features into new systems. In most organizations, there is generally neither a perceived reward for doing so, nor a penalty for not doing so.

Experience clearly indicates that data processing people *don't* recognize the problem. Even when they do, they often don't do a good job of building the controls into the systems. I believe that this is largely because management traditionally hasn't given the DP professional the necessary support, or the tools, to do a good job. Our colleges and universities aren't doing much to emphasize the importance of controls: As long as they churn out computer science and business data processing graduates who have never heard of internal accounting controls for applications, we are going to continue to be in big trouble. Organizations have reacted to the lack of internal controls in information systems by increasing the intensity of reviews by auditors (both independent and internal), quality assurance specialists, and others.

1.3 Application systems that fail

Besides failing to control assets, our application systems also fail to do what they are intended to do. Application systems should do what they are supposed to do — no more, no less. That sounds like a trivially obvious statement, but I assure you that it is not. Systems fail for one or more of these three reasons: missing functions, extra functions, and incorrect functions.

1.3.1 Missing functions

The first reason that systems fail to meet their intended goal is that *they don't perform the functions they are supposed to perform.* All too often, systems analysts and designers decide that they know more than the user does about what he needs. In the course of analysis, certain requested capabilities may be deemed "frivolous" by the data processing team and therefore omitted from the new system. Unfortunately, because traditional analysis tools (such as 2,500-page narrative specifications) are not easily understood by users, often the system is already installed before the user discovers that a request hasn't been implemented. When a non-implemented function turns out to be critical to the user, the system is judged to be (in part, at least) a failure.

That systems so often lack required functions can be regarded as a symptom of the need for more effective auditing of the product of systems analysis. While the auditor does get involved in auditing the functions of new systems, most installations cannot afford the luxury of having an independent audit of the development phase of every new system, because their auditing resources are limited.

Rather than blaming the audit, I believe that it is appropriate to blame the inability of traditional systems analysis and design techniques to produce models of the new system that the user can easily review. Clearly, there is limited benefit in the expenditure of scarce auditing resources to review ineffective products. Instead, the use of structured analysis for modeling a new system is, in and of itself, more powerful than any audit.* Through the use of improved tools for user/analyst

---

*For a good introduction to structured analysis techniques, see T. DeMarco's *Structured Analysis and System Specification* (New York: Yourdon Press, 1978).

communication and for system definition as offered by structured analysis techniques, systems can be designed to perform required functions without the need for intensive involvement by auditors. In the real world, the best reviewers of any new system are the users and systems developers themselves. After all, who knows the requirements or the new system better?

1.3.2 Extra functions

The second reason for failure is that *systems often perform functions they're not supposed to perform.* Sometimes, systems analysts give users *more* capabilities than users request, possibly to give the system "flexibility." Or, they may feel that the users "forgot" to ask for a capability that the users later would realize is needed. In the worst case, capabilities are built into systems without the user being told, either because they seem technically easy (or perhaps technically fascinating) to add, or because they will be some sort of a "surprise" for the user. Frequently, these added capabilities hinder or destroy the structure of the internal controls that the users and analysts worked hard to achieve.

For example, a massive payroll system was built with a secret "blunder fixing" routine. When normally blank fields of a specific control card were punched with certain codes, any field of any record on the master file could be modified without a log entry of any kind being created. When we stumbled across this feature during a security audit, the programmers acknowledged their creation. It was, they explained, a defense constructed to guard against the possibility of some unspecified disaster befalling the master file (perhaps lightning striking a power line and affecting the machine in mysterious ways). When asked why this capability was kept secret, the programmers replied that they built it in anticipation of an inevitable crisis. When it hit, they would surprise the user with an instant answer to the problem. We, on the other hand, saw it as a hole through which millions of dollars could be unlawfully directed.

Because excessive capabilities are likely to cause problems and because they consume resources (for design, implementation, debugging, and maintenance) that could be used for other projects, Cracker Jack® systems — systems with surprises inside — don't belong in business organizations. The presence of gratuitous capability is another symptom of inadequate analysis, and the use of structured analysis techniques can prevent this sort of analytic failure. As we'll see in Chapter 6, structured analysis gives the auditor a model, including documentation, of what the system should do, so that auditors can recognize secret routines. With non-structured specifications, it's difficult to know what the system is authorized to do.

1.3.3 Incorrect functions

The third and final reason that systems fail is that *they perform their intended functions incorrectly.* A system that incorrectly calculates salaries or credit card account interest, for example, is not desirable, to say the least. Like many other problems in systems development, incorrect performance of functions results from poor communication. It may be that the user did not properly communicate the correct procedures to the analyst, or that the analyst misunderstood the user. Perhaps the analyst built the model incorrectly, or the user could not detect the error because the model was too difficult to understand or was built with insufficient detail. The analyst may have incorrectly interpreted the user's critique of the model. Or, any of a dozen other communication problems could have occurred among users, analysts, designers, programmers, procedure writers, and others, thus causing the misunderstanding.

Remember, systems with defects that have not been detected prior to system installation are the most difficult and expensive to repair. Excess capability, missing functions, and performance errors represent, by definition, failures of quality control. If our quality control mechanisms worked flawlessly, there would be neither missing nor excess functions in our new systems, and all of the functions would work properly. But, sad to say, our experience clearly indicates that they don't.

1.3.4 Types of system errors: computer security failures

Many — probably most — systems have various built-in controls to avoid erroneous processing, but it's the failure, inadequacy, or absence of controls that leads to those 3:00 a.m. calls from the computer center: Before the system is built, auditors can help the analysts identify weaknesses in the error-avoidance controls. Specifically, they look for five types of errors: false negatives, false positives, destroyed data, incorrectly modified data, and compromised data.

The first type of error is *false negatives,* a term I've borrowed from the clinical laboratory. A false negative occurs when a test comes back negative that should have had a positive result. For example, a pregnancy test that indicates that a patient is not pregnant when in fact she is has a false negative result. In a data processing system, failure to reject a transaction that should not be processed is a false negative (for example, the "edits" in the program didn't detect the problem, and thus didn't raise the alarm when they should have). Some examples include a bank system that allows a withdrawal on an account that has neither a balance nor an overdraft privilege, or a system that accepts, for immediate shipment, a customer's order that requires out-of-stock items.

The opposite problem, *false positives,* occurs when the system rejects a transaction that should have been accepted. This happens when a condition is detected when none in fact exists; for example, a lab test indicates pregnancy in a non-pregnant woman, or even in a male patient. The relationship of false positives and false negatives to each other and to correct processing is shown in Figure 1.1.

SYSTEM'S ACTION

		Accept	Reject
	Accept	OK	False Positive
TRUE REQUIREMENT			
	Reject	False Negative	OK

Figure 1.1. The relationship of errors and correct processing.

False positives are particularly damaging to organizations when customer relations are involved. Consider, for example, that you find yourself on a Saturday night in desperate need of cash for some noteworthy purpose. You stroll over to your bank's nearest 24-hour automatic teller machine and insert your bank card. The machine courteously asks for your secret identification code number. You enter it correctly, and after a short delay, the display lights up with the following message:

INCORRECT CODE ENTERED.
YOUR CARD IS BEING HELD.
COME IN DURING BUSINESS HOURS
TO GET IT BACK.
GOODBYE.

As you can see from this bank example, rejecting correct inputs can be a problem, particularly when it impairs customer service or alienates the users within the organization.

The third type of error is *destroyed data.* Systems that irrevocably and improperly "lose" data from either transaction streams or files can destroy an organization's credibility, if not the organization itself. But data destruction can be a hidden problem . . . for a while. You, as the data processing manager, know you're in for a bad day when one of the users runs into your office and the following dialogue ensues:

USER: I have a question about the Frammis system that isn't covered in the user's manual. How do you un-delete a record on the system?

EDP: What's *un-delete* mean?

USER: Well, we need a way to change our mind after we tell the system to delete a customer's record.

EDP: When we built the system, you told us that deletes were final and irrevocable. Aren't they?

USER: Normally, yes. But this morning we discovered a problem. It seems that last week we meant to increase the credit limit for 5,000 of our key customers, but due to an error, we deleted the records instead.

EDP: How could you make that kind of an error 5,000 times?

USER: We didn't want to tell you, but our department acquired a small home computer, and someone programmed it to generate massive numbers of transactions and to simulate a dial-up terminal. We've been using it for two weeks now, but only today we discovered that it was programmed totally wrong. Whenever we try to increase a credit limit, the program initiates a delete transaction. Nothing serious, it just generates the wrong transaction code. Anyway, that's water under the bridge. When can you restore the 5,000 accounts?

EDP: I can't. We don't keep records of what you delete, because you never told us to. And we don't copy deleted records onto the back-up tape. I'm afraid the information is gone for good. Sorry.

USER: Sorry? Not as sorry as you'll be when we're through! How dare you build a system that doesn't keep an audit trail and copies of deleted records!

One point, of course, is that the need to recover deleted records always exists to some degree. Discovering the nature of the requirements in the systems you build is obviously part of your mission. You can't assume that a need doesn't exist simply because the user doesn't tell you about it. You've got to use informed, professional judgment.

Another way a system can go wrong is by producing *incorrectly modified data*. If your system tends to incorrectly modify records (either by changing the wrong record or incorrectly changing the right record) or if your logging (or lack of it) makes modifications to the data irrevocable, you are sitting on another powder keg. If the system can't protect the integrity, or the *correctness*, of the data, it may be worse than useless in the long run.

Consider the case of the computer service bureau that serviced the needs of some seventy small banks with no computers of their own. Every night, the banks sent their transactions to the service bureau, and every morning they received updated ledgers and customer balance listings. The checking account programs were always run on the second shift unless there was a problem. The general ledger programs, which balance each bank's books, ran on the third shift.

One night, the second-shift operator ran the checking account programs, but forgot to log the run. The third-shift operator, looking at the log, decided that there must have been problems on the second shift. He ran the checking programs again. Every deposit was therefore credited twice and every check was deducted from the customer's balance twice. That something had gone wrong was obvious when the general ledgers for all seventy banks were off by several million dollars. In addition, far more checks bounced than normal.

Unfortunately, the only records kept by the service bureau were the live, disk-based master files. There were no tape or disk back-ups of the files; and, as you have no doubt guessed, there was no program that could back out the second set of transactions from the checking account file.

So, for the three days it took to straighten the files, seventy small banks were forced to cash checks based not on recorded balances, but on faith. The word gets around fast: "Hey, Charlie! Did you hear that the 86th National Bank is cashing checks based on faith?"

"No, but let's get down there. I've got plenty of faith!" The service bureau closed shortly thereafter.

A fifth type of system error is *compromised data.* Hardly a week goes by without a news item or article about computers and privacy. Privacy is violated by compromise, by which I mean the unauthorized release — either accidental or deliberate — of the information processed or stored in a system.

Within your bank, for example, who should have access to data about your account? How about your credit records? Or your medical records? If a system doesn't have the necessary controls to limit access to the data to authorized persons only, it carries within it a malignancy just waiting to be activated by chance or by design.

Of course, not all of the controls that insure the confidentiality of data are automated. Often, careless distribution, handling, or discarding of confidential reports leads to a breakdown in security. People often forget that it's the simple things that can go wrong most easily.

1.4 Discovery of control failures

Eventually, management discovers weak controls in one of many ways (none of which are pleasant for the data processing department). In the following paragraphs, I'll discuss six kinds of events that signal to management the presence of inadequate controls.

Big disasters put the survival of the company at risk. How do you discover that your system has been sending out blank tapes as back-ups of the accounts receivable master file? Probably the first time the file fouls up and you try to restore it, you will discover that there is no back-up. How many of your customers will volunteer the amount they owe? How long will the company survive? If this occurs, be sure your resume is up-to-date.

Not-so-big disasters cost a company a lot of money, although it will survive. When management notices that your system has issued a $1,586,391.42 paycheck to cover two hours of overtime for a janitor, the managers are going to be very upset. You know the kind of questions they are going to ask: "How could this happen? Why didn't the controls catch this? Who's to blame for this?" I sincerely hope you've got some creative answers.

Embarrassment also can cost money and can be the worst type of exposure of all, because it has the highest probability of leading to just what organizations don't need — negative publicity. Examples are the municipal computer that files a lawsuit against a driver for unpaid parking tickets issued while the car in question could be proved to be thousands of miles away, or the bank computer that bounces a check on an account with sufficient funds.

Although *internal and external auditing reports* frequently point out control weaknesses in application systems, management often chooses (consciously or unconsciously) to ignore detailed auditing findings. Sometimes, the reports are written in technical terms, and aren't understandable by general managers. In other cases, the audit is not regarded as credible, for whatever reason, by the DP department. The data processing department often decries such reports as being unfair, incorrect, or non-objective (for example, the report is written to sell a particular consulting assignment). It doesn't particularly matter whether the charges are true or false, for their existence casts some doubt on the utility of the findings.

Fifth, management can learn about control weaknesses from *confessions*. Some of my best auditing findings over the years came not because of highly expert technical and esoteric auditing, but because someone confessed. For whatever reason (revenge, fear of discovery, or a desire to have one's case heard), management often finds someone to blow the whistle on severe weaknesses in controls. Sometimes, whistle blowers deserve and receive little credibility, but in other cases, they perform a valuable service to management by drawing attention to serious problems.

Last, management can resort to *sneaky methods.* Although I don't like to suggest that management ever uses less-than-ethical methods to find out things, I did hear of a case in which a manager devised a way to cause people to confess to problems they had been hiding. Here's how it is done: First, determine who it is you want to confess (the victim). Then, at 3:30 Friday afternoon, you (the boss) storm out of the office in an angry state. At 4:00, your secretary calls the victim and says, "The boss wants to see you in his office on Monday at 9:00 a.m. sharp. Be there!" When the victim asks what the meeting is all about, the secretary is instructed to say, "I don't know, but you saw how mad the boss was when he left. Could the meeting be related to his anger?" The victim has the weekend to think things over. On Monday, the victim is ushered into your office, and you say, "Well, what have you got to tell me?" Then you don't say another word. Within five minutes, I have been assured, most people will admit to *something*. It may not be everything, but it's a start.

1.5 Of managers, ostriches, and auditors

Yes, management eventually finds out, but did you ever wonder why it takes so long, and how system controls are permitted to deteriorate before remedial action is taken? I wondered. So, in an informal survey of nearly one hundred DP and general managers, I found that many were surprised to learn of their system's potential weaknesses, because they assumed that the data processing people were building effective controls into their systems. It's only when one of the untoward incidents listed above occurs that managers discover that their assumption was wrong.

Why did they make any assumption? The managers were accustomed to seeing controls in manual systems and figured that the DP people would do no less. Some managers reported that they had heard for years that computers were accurate, and had been told that if something went wrong, "The machine would stop and wouldn't process incorrect data." These assumptions were comforting, especially since technology was quickly changing the nature of data processing. When computers first arrived in the 1950s, managers were assured that they could always throw out the machine if it didn't work properly. By the mid-1960s, however, managers realized that this was no longer a choice, and that there was no alternative but to accept the computer's marvels. The banker knew there was no other practical way to manage and balance millions of accounts on a daily basis; the airline executive recognized that on-line reservation systems were a necessity for the airline business. Executives in industries from mining to manufacturing to refining came to see that, for better or worse, they were stuck with the infernal machines.

At the same time, managers realized that they were losing their understanding of these vital machines. As technology moved at an ever-increasing pace, systems became more complex, hardware became increasingly expensive, and new technical terms — *operating system, database, teleprocessing* — were more often heard. The combination of receding understanding and increasing dependency led management to pull back. The safest course, many managers felt, was to leave data processing alone, and to assume the best.

Data processing managers, meanwhile, didn't take long to detect this vacuum at the top, and they responded by telling management not to worry; given the right resources (usually hardware, software, and people), the ultimate system — integrating all major business functions — would be built. In a number of cases, the data processing staff members tried to pull it off: They jumped into the newest technology up to their eyeballs, to the benefit of the hardware manufacturers and, I suppose, to the benefit of technology in general. The only problem was that sometimes no effective applications were forthcoming. There were lots of research papers pushing the state of the art in, say, operating systems, but not much in the way of practical operations. When top management finally realized what was going on, it reacted by eliminating some of the DP managers involved.

1.6 Where we go from here

There is now, I think, more awareness by top managers that they have to take a more active role in managing their data processing resources. They have come to understand (usually the hard way) that part of their job is to make sure that the systems that are built do, in fact, have appropriate controls.

This book will tell you how to build internal controls into your systems, particularly those systems built using the techniques of structured systems development. While we can provide tools and techniques, the motivation to actually build well-controlled systems can't come from this or any other book. It's got to come from management, and extend throughout the systems development function and to the users.

Remember well: When you build information systems that affect assets, you are betting your business. That kind of a bet deserves the insurance of internal controls.

2 | Auditing Tasks and Auditing Specialists

What do EDP auditors do? Specifically, what tasks do they perform and which control specialists perform them? How does the use of structured systems development techniques have any effect on auditing or internal controls in application systems? Those are the questions we'll be answering in this chapter.

In reading this chapter, keep one concept firmly in mind: The functions of an EDP auditor don't necessarily have to be performed by people who bill themselves as EDP auditors or as other control specialists. The key to successful internal control is *not* in the hands of these people, but rather in the hands of a generalist, the systems developer.

By definition, an audit or review is an *ex post facto* function. Auditors review work that has already been accomplished. So, if a problem is found in the course of a review, it requires corrective work — another phrase meaning maintenance. The only reliable, predictable way to minimize control-related maintenance is to build control into the system in the first place.

I am suggesting that you as a systems developer play the role of auditor and consciously review your work for compliance with control requirements while you are doing it. Of course, to be your own auditor, you must first understand what auditing means. In addition, you must understand what auditors do.

2.1 What does "how to audit" mean?

When auditors discuss *how to audit* any business process, they use that phrase to include two different decisions. First, they must decide on an auditing strategy. In the case of EDP systems, auditors talk in terms of "auditing around" versus "auditing through" the computer.

If the auditor believes (and this belief must be based on a thorough examination of the system) that the system has adequate controls, that those controls are operating properly, and that the computer operations environment is properly controlled, he can rely on the outputs of the system for auditing purposes. This approach is called auditing *through* a system. When the auditor isn't convinced of the completeness or reliability of the controls, then the auditor can't rely on the outputs, and must audit *around* the system.

For example, consider a bank's program that calculates interest on savings accounts. If the auditor examines the system and determines that it has the necessary controls to calculate interest properly, and has adequate error detection and reporting capabilities, then he can rely on the validity of a tape of interest payments produced by the system. If the controls necessary for reliance aren't there, however, then the work of the system must be reverified, usually through an appropriate statistical sampling technique. In the banking case, the auditor would have to take a large, statistically selected sample from the tape, match the records to the inputs, and manually verify the correctness of the calculations.

Second, having decided on a strategy, the auditor must decide on the particular audit tests to be used to implement the strategy. In the example above, the auditor used statistical sampling to implement his decision to audit around the system. Frequently, various statistical sampling techniques are also used to audit through a system. There are at least a dozen excellent software packages to assist the auditor in carrying out the audit's sampling function. Knowledge of both auditing and statistical sampling is required to properly select a sample, and to select the proper tests (for example, the use of positive versus negative balance confirmations*). Failure to make these selections properly can cast doubt on the results obtained in the audit. No packaged software can provide the professional knowledge to make these judgments, so it is important to recognize that the various EDP auditing support packages are nothing more than *tools* that assist the auditor.

Positive confirmations are those that the auditor wants returned whether the balance shown is correct or incorrect. In the case of *negative* confirmations, the auditor wishes to receive only those confirmations indicating an error.

2.2 What do EDP auditors do?

There is no single listing of major functions performed by EDP auditors that is universally accepted. (Of course, the same is true for systems analysis functions.) A list that is widely accepted and is based upon a great deal of empirical data about the field of EDP auditing consists of eleven major functions, as briefly described below:*

- *Application systems control review:* a review of controls in the installed application system to determine that it produces information in a timely, accurate, and complete manner. This type of review is often performed by external auditors in conjunction with the annual financial audit.[†] By definition, an application systems control review can be conducted only on a system that has already been implemented.

- *Data integrity review:* a review of a file of data for completeness, consistency, and correctness.

- *Systems development life cycle review:* a review of an organization's standards for conducting every phase of the systems development life cycle to determine whether the standards, if followed, would result in a complete, well-designed, and well-documented system. Of course, auditors ought to integrate structured methods into their conception of generally accepted standards for the systems development life cycle.

---

*This list is based on the EDP Auditors Foundation for Education and Research (EDPAF). It has been adopted by EDPAF's Professional Certification Board as the basis for the EDP auditors' certification examination.
[†]The purpose of the annual financial audit of a company is to determine whether the balance sheets, income statements, and accompanying notes fairly represent the organization's financial status. However, because the auditor's review is brief, it is often possible to build a false front of controls in key systems and fool the auditor into placing too much confidence in the accuracy and reliability of the system. To do so is, of course, unwise, unprofessional, and possibly illegal! This annual review process, which also includes a review of the data processing installation, is sometimes referred to as an SAS3 Review. SAS3 stands for the Statement on Auditing Standards Number 3, a rule of the American Institute of CPAs requiring a review of EDP systems prior to placing reliance on them in an audit.

- *Application development review:* a review of systems under development in order to determine the adequacy and completeness of planned controls and, if necessary, to recommend additional controls. From the systems analyst's viewpoint, the auditor becomes another user during this review, but not *just another* user. The auditor's control requirements can span the domains of all users of the system, and reach across both sides of the man-machine boundary.

  Ideally, the auditor reviews the system under development during both the analysis phase (to determine *what* controls are needed) and the design phase (to determine *how* to implement those controls). As with any other user requirement, the earlier in the life cycle control requirements are specified, the easier it is to include them in the new system's design. Unfortunately, many systems don't undergo auditing reviews until they enter systems testing or even until after they are operational. Then, the changes that the auditors insist upon can lead to months or years of remedial work. It is clearly to everyone's advantage to have auditing controls built into the system right from the start. Remember that auditability is a basic requirement of every business system. It follows, then, that one of the basic objectives of the systems development process must be to build auditable systems.* Why not do so as efficiently as possible by auditing early in the life cycle?

- *General operational procedures control review:* a review of both the data processing operating procedures and the actual operations to determine if applications are processed in a controlled environment. In this review, the auditor looks at the general controls in an installation in order to determine whether performing an application systems control review would be a waste of time and effort. If the installation's controls are poor, it

---

*An auditable system differs from one with proper auditing controls in that a system may, in fact, have terrific controls, but may be so poorly documented as to make it impossible to audit. Auditability refers to the characteristic of being easily reviewed.

doesn't matter whether a particular application's controls are good. The results of systems that are run in a poorly controlled installation cannot be relied upon for auditing purposes, and it becomes necessary to audit around the computer.

The review consists of two stages: First, the auditor determines whether the company's procedures, such as documentation standards, are being complied with. For example, if policy calls for use of a sign-out log to control delivery of blank checks from storage to the computer room, the auditor would determine whether the log exists, and whether it is used as intended. Second, the auditor determines whether the company's control standards are reasonable in light of what are called "generally accepted standards." For example, failure to have a policy to control access to blank checks is unacceptable. The auditor is expected to report such problems to corporate management.

- *Security review:* a review of the system's security methods and procedures in order to assure the appropriate protection of programs, data, and the data processing installation from accidental or deliberate destruction, modification, or compromise.

- *Systems software review:* a review of the controls over and within the systems software to determine compliance with the organization's policy. For example, is there a policy for control over modifications to operating systems, DBMS, SORTS, communication software, and utilities? If so, how are the modifications implemented? If no policy exists, the auditor must review the safeguards that protect the organization from unauthorized changes.

- *Maintenance review:* a review of the process of modifying existing systems to determine that they are being altered in accordance with the organization's policies. Given the statistics showing the high percentage of total systems lifetime cost devoted to maintenance, this review is considered to be one of the most important.

- *Acquisition review:* a review of the process of acquiring services (for example, telecommunications, staffing, and training), hardware, and software in order to determine if the organization's resources are being used economically.

- *Data processing resource management review:* a review of the data processing department's planning, administrative, and management practices in order to determine their adequacy in fulfilling the organization's goals.

- *Information systems auditing management:* planning and organizing the auditing function to assure maximum use of the available resources to fulfill the organization's auditing needs.

While all of these reviews may be performed by professional auditors, a wide variety of specialists may be involved in them. Remembering my caution at the beginning of this chapter — that all of these reviews need not be performed by auditors only — let's now turn to consider the different specialists you're likely to encounter.

2.3 A who's who of EDP control specialists

There are five general categories of specialists who may be involved in a systems development project: external auditors, internal auditors, quality control specialists, computer security specialists, and risk managers. I'll explain the skills and responsibilities of each in the following sections.

2.3.1 External (independent) auditors

All large companies and many smaller ones engage firms of certified public accountants or chartered accountants to conduct reviews of their financial records. Likewise, virtually every governmental unit is subject to reviews by various auditing bodies, many of which operate independently of the agencies they audit. For example, in the United States government, the General Accounting Office conducts reviews of federal agencies and reports directly to Congress.

The purpose of the traditional *balance sheet* audit performed by independent auditors is simply to render an opinion whether the financial statements (balance sheets, income statements, and so forth) fairly represent the company's fiscal position. By "fair representation," auditors mean that the statements do not contain misstatements of a "material" nature, are prepared in accordance with generally accepted accounting practices, and contain appropriate notes.

When auditors certify financial statements, they do not mean that the statements are correct to the penny. Rather, they are stating that nothing came to the auditor's attention to suggest that the figures are materially incorrect. Clearly, in huge companies with balance sheet totals measured in tens of billions of dollars, there is no way for the auditors to review every transaction or every dollar.

Auditors perform this function (which is called the *attest* function) by reviewing and verifying various records. Obviously, companies have adopted more and more sophisticated computer-based record-keeping systems. Thus, larger proportions of the records that the auditors must review now pass through the data processing department. This has resulted in tremendous growth in the need to conduct reviews of the data processing function.

In reviewing the systems that their clients use for financial record-keeping, external auditors are charged with determining whether sufficient controls are built into the systems to insure the reliability of the outputs of the systems and whether those controls work properly. This review of internal controls is generally conducted each year, and consists of two phases:

- *General operational procedures control review:* The auditors first review the overall operation of the data processing department to determine if a "controlled environment" exists. They must find out whether the standards governing security, documentation, systems development, and operations, among others, are present and whether the implementation of those standards permits the controls in a well-designed system to operate correctly.

  For example, if balancing errors detected by an application system are ignored by computer operations, the control built into the system is defeated. Indeed, the auditor would find that it didn't matter whether controls were in the applications, since the poor operating environment nullifies the application controls. If the general controls are satisfactory, then the auditor can proceed with the review.

- *Application systems control review:* Second, the external auditor looks at selected applications that are key to the audit, including general ledger, accounts payable, accounts receivable, and payroll. The auditor determines whether the application under review contains sufficient controls to insure that the data are processed properly.

When conducting these reviews, external auditors work directly with the data processing department. Problems often appear in the relationship. Since the auditors typically have few hours available to do their work, the DP staff can avoid friction by providing the information and assistance required as efficiently as possible. Auditors, too, must work with DP when errors are discovered; auditors should carefully review proposed comments with the DP people prior to reporting them to upper management.

Independent auditing firms also conduct other kinds of reviews, for example, of systems development, security, and performance measurement. However, in conducting these reviews, the auditing firms are acting as consultants, and we shall consider these as not being unique external auditing tasks. Rather, they are equivalent to similar tasks performed by internal auditors and quality control specialists.

2.3.2 Internal auditors

Internal auditors, as the name implies, are employed by the company they audit. They generally report to a senior officer of the company or, in some cases, to the audit committee of the board of directors. Because they are on the company's payroll (as opposed to external auditors, who receive high per-diem payments), they can spend more time on their reviews and examine more detailed records. In most cases, internal EDP auditors have the same professional qualifications as do their colleagues in public accounting firms, but they also have the in-depth knowledge of company operations that comes from having only one client.

Internal EDP auditors frequently perform a wider range of reviews than do external auditors; they generally perform all of the types of review described in Section 2.2. Unfortunately, even the internal auditor is often treated by DP people as an outsider, not to be trusted and not to be called in voluntarily. (See Section 2.4.) Most of you, whether auditor, DP staff member, or manager, can testify from personal experience that this statement is undeniably true. For years, I've thought about the problem, and can offer only these observations: If you as the internal auditor define those who are audited as "clients" or "subjects" rather than as "colleagues," you're on the way to trouble. Colleagues work *with* their fellows to achieve some mutual goal. The alternative is to work *on* your subject, client, or victim.

If the internal auditors or DP personnel consciously set up adversary relationships during audits, you've already got trouble.* Hostile, adversary-based reviews waste time, work, and resources. Proper auditing procedures do not require an adversary relationship — just independence. I've always found that working with my clients (rather than on them) resulted in a better, more accurate, more cost-effective review.

If a cooperative, helping relationship can be established between the internal auditors and the DP staff, the result is more effective systems with better controls. And the controls can be built in efficiently as part of the original system design, as we'll see in Chapter 7.

One way in which the positive relationships can be strengthened is through shared training. For example, to choose a subject somewhat close to my heart, consider training in structured systems development. When your organization sponsors a course or sends DP employees to a seminar, do the EDP auditors ever attend? They should. How else can they learn the techniques that they are expected to audit? When the auditors attend conferences on such subjects as internal control or computer security, do they invite representatives of the DP department to join them? They should attend, too.

2.3.3 Quality control/quality assurance specialists

Quality control or quality assurance specialists are experts in internal control and error detection and work within data processing departments. They generally divide their time between conducting formal and informal reviews, and serving as consultants or advisors to project managers. If, for historical, political, or neurotic reasons, the DP staff members fear or distrust the auditors, who can they look to for advice concerning internal controls?

Many organizations have analyzed the problem as follows: Generally, DP professionals simply don't like anyone who has the role of a consultant. But what seems to bother them most about auditors is their attitude of absolute independence: the attitude, as one DP director put it, of being "better than the technicians, of believing that their role is to enlighten the heathen savages of the DP department." He went on to add, "Besides, auditors are finks. They find a problem and right

---

*Don't worry about the effect of an adversary environment on the ongoing relationship between the DP staff and the auditors when actual fraud or other malfeasant activity is suspected. In such a case, the continuing relationship between the DP staff and the auditors won't matter. In all other cases, however, those people who cause the adversity — and they can exist on both the auditing and DP staffs — do their organizations a gross injustice.

away the world, or at least top management, knows all about it. Shouldn't DP management have the option of knowing the problems before everyone else finds out?''

So what the organizations have done is to find people with many of the same qualifications as EDP auditors, and to assign them to the DP department. As internal consultants, they must still counter the resistance offered by the project managers to any consultant. But at least they are recognized as being part of the DP team. They can be told of problems and can be consulted without the DP department's having to worry about the dirty linen being aired in public.

When work volumes permit, organizations can afford a full-time quality control/quality assurance specialist. Unfortunately, these specialists face a deadend in their career path. Their experience is often not seen as qualifying them for DP management or for project management positions, and they may be viewed as "traitors" by some misguided auditors.*

The QC/QA specialist represents a resource to be used by each project manager. Working with the QC/QA person, systems developers can build an internal control plan as an integrated part of the development of the system itself.

2.3.4 Computer security specialists

Computer security is in the news. It is hard to pick up a DP journal without reading reports of computer frauds and crimes, and of new tools to foil such nefarious goings-on. With the growing attention focused on the security issue, there has been a similar increase in the number of people who call themselves computer security specialists. These specialists conduct security reviews. Unfortunately, there is no generally accepted definition of just what a security review is.

Over the past few years, I've been privileged to work with some of the finest and most professional people in this field. But I've also had to put up with some of the unprofessional charlatans who have jumped, quite profitably, onto the security bandwagon. The difference

---

*Please don't write to me to complain that I am painting an unjustified image of auditors. There are, sadly, a number of EDP auditors and auditing managers who *do* treat internal QC/QA people like second-class citizens, just as there are unprofessional independent auditors who treat internal auditors like less-than-adequate human beings. I'm not attacking the auditing profession, but simply pointing out that auditors with these attitudes are not representative of the auditing industry. Such persons are incompetent and unprofessional, and should be recognized as such.

between them was, in essence, that the charlatans were ready to sell a solution without diagnosing the problem. Even if they did ask, they didn't listen to the reply. They were selling *the* answer, which usually revolved around some sort of physical security device, or some miraculous software package touted as solving all of your computer control and security problems. Often, this sort of sophisticated gadgetry is better suited to James Bond than to John and Jane Q. Programmer.

In the vast majority of cases, including such security-sensitive industries as banks, brokerage houses, and insurance companies, I estimate that physical security represents no more than ten percent of the problem of controlling the information resource. Defending against errors and omissions, largely through intelligently designed internal application system controls, is far more important in the long run. But internal controls are not glamorous; management is more impressed by such physical security devices as badge-operated locks, hand geometry readers, and fingerprint scanners. While such physical security devices are valuable and some even necessary, as in the case of fire detection and suppression systems, a real danger lies in the ease with which companies rely completely on such obvious measures, and ignore the truly significant safeguards. Regard with suspicion any so-called security expert who tells you that physical security is the most important factor in controlling your information resources, and who fails to discuss the importance of internal application controls.

The good professional security consultants and internal specialists recognize the importance of built-in controls and can go a long way toward helping you build a balanced security program. Overreliance on external controls, however, can lead you to rely on a facade of security with no more substance than the false houses of a motion picture set.

2.3.5 Risk management specialists

Insurance is another, lesser-known component of DP control and security and has its own type of specialist. Risk managers are specialists in evaluating the need for insurance coverage, and in evaluating available policies to obtain the greatest coverage at the lowest cost for their employers. Insurance contracts covering the information resource are complex and are becoming more so. Understanding the various options available is vital if you are to avoid catastrophes such as losing a master file in a fire and discovering that the company's fire policy covered only the replacement of the media on which the file was written. Rather than collecting the $200,000 needed to recreate the file, you receive a blank reel of tape and the best wishes of the insurance company.

Risk managers work closely with DP management and security specialists to analyze the risks associated with the information management operations, and to develop a program of insurance coverage that makes sense in light of other control and security measures that the organization is taking. There are three sources of such risk management expertise. In large organizations, the corporate insurance department may have a staff member with special knowledge in the area of EDP insurance. A second source is the large insurance brokerage houses, of which there are many. And, of course, the major insurance carriers have experts on their staffs who can at least explain the various risks covered by insurance.

2.4 How are EDP auditors perceived?

There are far fewer EDP internal control specialists than there are data processing people. Indeed, ratios of five hundred to one or more are not unusual. It is remarkable that, given their small numbers, they could have any significant effect, but they do. Even more amazing, other data processing people perceive these people as threatening, or as trespassing on DP's turf. This defensive attitude is tragic for two reasons: Wishing won't make them go away; and second, they can offer much good advice on control. Ignoring the auditors and other control specialists won't cause them to fold up their tents and steal away into the night — quite the contrary. They have an important job to do: to improve the level of control built into the systems, both manual and automated. As many data processing managers have learned too late, trying to work at cross-purposes to auditors and other control specialists can be unhealthy to one's career.

I remember the case of a vice president of data processing in a major corporation who refused to cooperate in his department's review by the external auditors. The presence of the auditors, he felt, was an insult to him. He had been doing a good job for years, and didn't see any need to have "outsiders" waste his time. As he saw it, it came down to a choice by top management between him and the auditors. Top management agreed. It fired him.

In another case, an insurance company was considering the purchase of a computer security audit. Uncertain of the need for the study, the board of directors called in the senior vice president who supervised the data processing department to ask for his opinion. "It's a waste of money," he responded. "We've got all the bases covered in security. We've bought the best, most expensive security systems. We worry about it day and night. The auditors aren't going to find anything wrong, so why bother?" The board chairman replied, "Look, I agree that they're probably going to find nothing, but I've got to be concerned about anyone who tells me that he's doing such a good job that there's no need to check on him. Checking up on everything in this company is our responsibility to the stockholders." The board ordered the security audit, which my colleagues and I performed. We indeed discovered significant weaknesses.

In today's business environment, reviews and audits are a fact of life. The more control a department has over assets, the more closely that department is going to be watched. So if you can't get rid of the reviews, or the reviewers, what's your alternative?

Ignoring or fighting the auditors is wasteful because their knowledge can improve your systems. The specialists are a major source of good advice on control. Instead of looking at reviews as interference or abuse, why not reverse the relationship and seek advice? Problems found in reviews conducted after a system is built, or even at the end of a life cycle phase, are difficult and often expensive to go back and fix, especially if, as sometimes happens, the installation of the controls involves an almost complete re-design. But if the advice of specialists in control is sought *before* the work is done or, at the latest, while the work is being done, the controls will evolve as an integral part of the system. I'm not saying that it is easy to invite new players onto the design team either as members or advisors, only that it is smart to do so, and will minimize control-related aggravation.

From the DP manager's viewpoint, the task of the auditors (with whom DP *must* interact) appears to be the generation of unnecessary aggravation. The auditors are quick to criticize; they're frequently not up-to-date with the technologies and methodologies used in the DP installation (including structured analysis and design); and, perhaps worst of all, their reports go directly to the board of directors and to top management, who demand answers. All in all, from the DP department's viewpoint, the auditing process can be a pain in the neck. You don't have to look far to find a DP person with a horror story concerning EDP auditing.*

2.4.1 An auditor's tales of horror

A common problem DPers have with auditors is that auditing procedures don't keep pace with systems development advances, and auditors have rigid preconceptions or, worse, absolutely no understanding of phased development. Consider the case of the purported EDP auditor who shows up during the company's annual financial audit. The auditor looks about fifteen years old, and immediately provides ample evidence that he (or she) is utterly incapable of distinguishing between a

---

*Parts of this section originally appeared in an article entitled "Auditors' Tales of Horror," *The YOURDON Report*, Vol. 6, No. 4 (July-September 1981), pp. 2, 5-6. Copyright © 1981 by YOURDON inc.

computer and a photocopier. As the DP manager, you humor the auditor. You and your staff spend the better part of a week answering questions that appear to come from a printed checklist that the auditor has none too cleverly concealed in his notebook.

Some questions appear reasonable. For example, you can understand why an auditor might want to know when and how you provide back-up copies of your documentation. Other questions don't seem to make much sense: all those questions about program flowcharts and narrative descriptions of systems, for example. You explain that neither long narratives nor traditional flowcharts are used in the documentation of structured analyses and designs, but the auditor continues asking about them. You wonder why, decide that you'll never understand auditors, and go on to another topic.

Several weeks later, you are called into your boss's office to review the auditor's report (often referred to as a "management letter"). You can't believe it. It bears no relationship to reality. The things in your shop that you *know* are problems are ignored in the report, and things that you know are in great shape are totally blasted. Some pieces of the report seem to come directly from outer space.

How could the auditors have told the board of directors that your documentation standards are unacceptable because you don't have traditional systems and program flowcharts, and because your systems analysis process doesn't result in a 5,000-page narrative (what Tom DeMarco calls a Victorian novel specification*)? And, how could the same auditor have written a scathing denunciation of your practice of not showing detailed processing of trivial rejects on your data flow diagrams? Don't these auditors understand what structured analysis and design are all about?

Here's another all too familiar tear-jerker that illustrates the common disparity in scheduling and work priorities between the auditors and the systems developers. You are rolling along into the testing of your new whiz-bang system. Suddenly, the internal auditor, whom you've been trying to see for five months, appears to announce that your request to see him has finally reached the top of the audit department's work queue.

The subsequent audit of the controls in your system reveals that the controls are totally inadequate. Extensive changes are required, including new and modified dataflows, modified data stores, new bubbles, and new reports. The following dialogue ensues:

---

*T. DeMarco, *Structured Analysis and System Specification* (New York: Yourdon Press, 1978), p. 13.

EDP: Why didn't you tell us about the problems before?

AUDIT: We're telling you now.

EDP: We put every accounting control that was in the old system into our new system.

AUDIT: Big deal. The old system had lousy controls. I thought everyone knew that.

EDP: And every new control that the users specified is 100 percent operational.

AUDIT: Those users weren't professional auditors. They aren't qualified to know if their controls are adequate or not. You should have asked us.

EDP: We did. You were too busy to work with us, remember?

AUDIT: You hit us at the height of the busy season: fiscal year-end, external auditors running all over the place! But we've got plenty of time now.

EDP: Swell.

AUDIT: So let's start at the beginning and see if we can salvage anything. By the way, I saw the external auditor's management letter on your department. Not too good, was it? How can you expect to build a good system if you can't even put together an acceptable system narrative?

EDP: Aaarrgghhh!

Understand that I'm not laying all of the blame for the horror stories on the auditors; far from it. Data processing people have more than their share of sins to answer for, too. Have you as a DP manager ever introduced a methodology that you knew would significantly change the way in which your organization builds new systems without making your organization's EDP auditors a part of the decision making process? Of course, even in those cases in which the auditors are aware of the changes contemplated by the data processing people, the auditors aren't told, for example, *how* to audit a structured specification. We tell them what it is, and assume that they can take it from there. That is a bad assumption to make.

In short, the function that auditors perform is the review of systems to determine whether the assets controlled by the system are properly safeguarded. To perform such reviews, the auditor must understand the tools and techniques used by the development team for the particular system. Obviously, an auditor cannot review a document he cannot read. If the auditor were assigned to review a system that was documented in Japanese, clearly he would be unable to proceed without first learning Japanese. A more dangerous situation occurs when the problem is not so obvious. Such is the case of the auditor having no knowledge of structured techniques.

2.5 How do the structured techniques affect EDP auditing?

If the use of structured techniques didn't have any effect on EDP auditing, this book would have never been written. But before I can really discuss the effects, it is vital to review three key underlying assumptions about EDP auditing in general:

- The need for controls in EDP systems exists regardless of the analysis and design methodologies employed.

- The specific internal accounting control techniques available for use in the system should not depend on the methodology selected.

- The way in which controls are defined and documented is dependent on the rules of the particular methodology used.

Let's discuss these assumptions through a simple case study, which concerns a particular set of controls in an order entry process. Here's an excerpt from the policy of XYZ, Inc.:

Batch Control of Sales Tickets

In order to insure that all sales are entered and that all salespersons receive commissions promptly, the following rules apply: First, there will be one batch of sales tickets per day per salesperson. Second, each salesperson will prepare a batch ticket to be submitted with completed sales tickets. (This will include the salesperson's six-digit employee number, which includes a check digit; the number of sales tickets submitted, including voided sales tickets; and the dollar and cents total of all valid orders in the batch.) Third, if either the employee number is invalid or the count is wrong or the dollar total is wrong, the accounting office will reject the batch and return it to the salesperson. This will delay commission payments, and should motivate the salespeople to submit correct tickets.

This policy was given to XYZ's data processing department for use in building XYZ-IFMS, the company's Integrated Financial Management System.

Let's consider the controls on this process in the new system, given that we don't know anything about the XYZ data processing department's standards for systems design. The policy statement implies the following controls in order to assure proper processing of sales ticket inputs:

1. The system should accept only one batch per salesperson per day.

2. Each batch must be accompanied by a batch record.

3. The employee number on the batch record must bear a proper check digit and the valid number of a current salesperson.

4. The sales ticket count entered on the batch ticket must be equal to the number of tickets, both valid and invalid, in the batch.

5. The dollar total entered on the batch ticket must be equal to the sum of the dollar values of valid sales tickets in the batch.

6. If any one of the first five rules is violated, reject the entire batch.

We want at least these six components of internal control to be built into the new system regardless of the design methodology used. A basic rule of systems development, both manual and automated, is that any system that affects an asset or major process of the organization must be subject to internal accounting controls. By "accounting controls" I mean the policies, records, procedures, and methods that protect the organization's assets and ensure the accuracy and completeness of the organization's records. These controls must provide what is called "reasonable assurance" that transactions that affect assets are properly authorized and recorded, that the organization's assets are safeguarded, and that the records can be fully reviewed (audited) on a regular basis.

Of course, the key concept, *reasonable,* is open to interpretation. What is reasonable control to me might be interpreted as insufficient control by a second observer, or too much control by a third. The degree of control required for a particular aspect of a system must be agreed upon, as early in the systems development life cycle as possible, by the systems designer, the user, and the auditor.

The question of how much control is a sensitive one, because it represents a trade-off. The more control, the more complexity in the system. There is some point at which the controls become so extensive that they are unworkable, in terms of cost, throughput, or interface requirements. In later chapters, as we discuss the techniques of building controls into systems, you'll see the alternatives for greater or lesser control and how to communicate those alternatives to the user.

The requirement for internal accounting control is a function of the underlying business process, not of the fact that the process is to be automated. This point is important. Too many DP professionals believe that controls are put into systems to placate the auditors. Nothing can be further from the truth. Controls are put into systems to protect the assets.

Earlier, we asserted that the use of the structured techniques affects EDP auditing. Clearly, in order to accomplish the major auditing tasks properly, the auditor must understand how controls work and are documented in a structured analysis and design environment. Table 2.1 shows which types of review are affected. The paragraphs following the table provide an explanation of how each task is affected.

Table 2.1
Impact of Structured Analysis and Design
on Major EDP Auditing Tasks

DIRECTLY AFFECTED	NOT DIRECTLY AFFECTED
1. Application Systems Control Review	2. Data Integrity Review
3. Systems Development Life Cycle Review	5. General Operational Procedures Control Review
4. Application Development Review 6. Security Review	7. Systems Software Review
8. Maintenance Review	9. Acquisition Review
11. Information Systems Auditing Management	10. Data Processing Resource Management Review

To properly perform an *application systems control review* in a structured environment, the auditor must understand the graphic and text tools used in the structured methodologies, and particularly the way in which application controls are specified within the techniques. The development staff, in addition, requires an understanding of the internal controls available for use; of particular importance is the new evaluation technique — phase-related control — introduced in Chapter 5. This technique enables the auditor or systems designer to classify controls into three groups: those that should be specified in the analysis phase; those that should be specified in the design phase; and those that should not be specified until the implementation phase. This unique analytic tool allows for minimal constraint in the design of systems while still assuring adequate levels of control.

The *systems development life cycle review* obviously requires an understanding of the systems development techniques used in the organization. There are significant differences between the structured and traditional life cycles, and these are discussed in Chapter 3 from both the viewpoint of the systems developer and of the auditor.

As with the application systems control review, the *application development review* requires both knowledge of the tools of structured analysis and design and knowledge of audit and control tools applicable to each stage of an application's development.

The *security review* in the structured systems development environment also requires knowledge of the tools of structured development. The structured methodology is well suited to the development of system security schemas during application development.

One of the major benefits of structured methodologies is the improvement seen in system maintenance efficiency. By reducing redundancy and providing efficient descriptive tools, structured methods change the way maintenance is accomplished. In a *maintenance review,* the auditor must understand these changes in order to conduct an effective audit of the maintenance process.

The sum of these changes in auditing techniques for the structured systems development environment has an impact on *information systems auditing management.* First, the manager must take into account the training needed to properly prepare auditing staff members to perform in the new environment. Second, the manager must assess the impact of these changes on scheduling of audits. Phase-related control, the new technique for control classification, will significantly increase the return on audit hours spent during analysis and design of new systems. By being able to conduct reviews to determine that the *right* control is developed at the *right* point in the development life cycle, the auditor can do a more effective job of assuring proper controls while not unnecessarily interfering in the systems development process.

2.6 Summary

In this chapter, we've reviewed the tasks that EDP auditors perform, and the various specialists involved in the EDP auditing process. We've also reviewed the effect of the structured tools and techniques on auditing tasks.

In summary, remember that, in spite of the effects of the structured techniques, the net result can be no different: We must still achieve effective internal control and auditability of the systems we develop.

3 | EDP Auditing and the Systems Development Life Cycle

In the traditional systems development life cycle, auditing of DP systems occurs at a formal checkpoint at the end of each phase of development. At that time, both auditors and DP professionals review and criticize the system before work begins on the next phase. The concept is simple and straightforward and the procedure permits reviews with a minimum use of the scarce auditing resource. It also offers the possibly antagonistic DP staff members a limited, scheduled interaction with the auditor. However, the traditional systems development life cycle and the auditing methodologies that relate to it are based on a latter-day fairy tale:

> Once upon a time, there was a project leader who undertook the development of a wondrous new information system. At the end of the General Design Phase, he stopped. He called in other wise men and women — users, auditors, and the like — to praise his handiwork. They found his work pleasing, so they blessed the project, signed the Official Sign-Off Form, and bade him to proceed with haste.
>
> So he did. He labored diligently until he reached the end of the Detailed Design Phase. Once again, he called in the others to heap praises and to sign off on the system.
>
> They did. So he undertook programming and testing, and in due season implemented his oft-signed-off system. And everyone lived happily ever after.

I call the traditional life cycle a fairy tale because although it is based on a premise that is conceptually valid, it is unworkable in real life. The premise is that most, if not all, of any given phase of systems development must be completed, and everyone must sign off on the phase, before the next phase begins. Once a phase is done, it is not modified until the system is implemented. This approach to systems development is called *conservative* development.

Unfortunately, the pressure to complete systems quickly, the need to correct errors found during the development process, and the desire to implement systems one part at a time make it unrealistic and often impossible to proceed in a neat, phase-by-phase fashion. We need life cycles and auditing techniques that are flexible: They must be able to accommodate feedback between development phases, and changes to functional requirements throughout development; they also must allow simultaneous performance of tasks from two or more development phases. This kind of life cycle is called *radical* development.

To convince the cynical readers of the need for a nontraditional SDLC, I'll present two real-world examples. Assume, as a systems developer, that you are busily involved in design when you discover an error made during the analysis phase and overlooked by the reviewers. If you ignore the problem, you aren't really doing your job (which is to build the right system). If you blame it on the reviewers (or users or auditors or anyone else), you haven't solved the problem; you've only made political waves. If you decide to treat the problem as a requirement statement for a future system enhancement, you've just guaranteed that you're going to build, test, and implement the wrong system. Your system will be obsolete before it is built. If you go back and fix it, you'll be violating the traditional life cycle concept of sign-offs. That is, if you make the change, you'll have to go through the phase-end sign-off process all over again. And if you do that, you'll have to take the blame for delaying the project and for poor planning.

Or, to take another example, assume that a user tells you that he's changed his mind and decided that new functions X and Z should be performed in a somewhat different way, and should result in slightly different report formats than were previously specified. What do you do? You obviously can't ignore the user's changes. (A user rightfully gets mad when he hears about "frozen" specifications.) If you tell him that you'll handle it as another post-installation enhancement, he'll recognize it as a DP smoke screen. (After all, users get lots of practice: The typical large DP shop generates more smoke screens in a month than did both sides in World War II.) Obviously, grumbling doesn't help. You should change the specification. You may not like to make these corrections, but since such changes happen all the time, you might as well get used to them.

User policy is always in some state of flux. As a result, information systems (even new ones still under development) are also in a state of flux, a condition that leads to one of the basic realities of systems development:

> *Rule:* If the user changes the rules, you must change the system to meet the new rules.

You don't have to like it, but it's mighty hard to defend the installation of an obsolete (that is, wrong) system. (The short form of this rule is, *Frozen specs aren't!)*

There are primarily two problems with the traditional SDLC: one-way doors between phases and no phase overlap (see Figure 3.1).

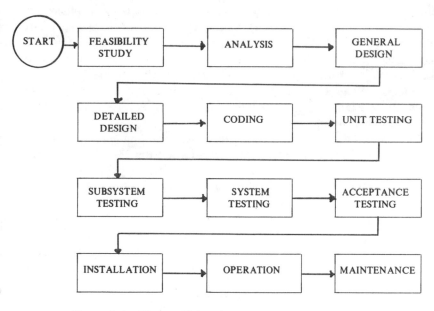

Figure 3.1. The traditional systems development life cycle.

The phases of the traditional systems development life cycle imply a linear, sequential progression from phase to phase. At any given time, you are at one and only one place in the cycle. This concept also inspired the sign that was on my third-grade classroom door:

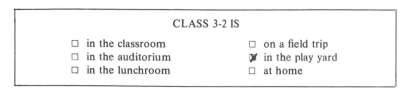

Figure 3.2. A good way to keep track of a third-grade class.

That's a fine way to keep track of a group of third-graders, but I don't think it's a realistic way to keep track of a large-scale systems development project. Imagine the following:

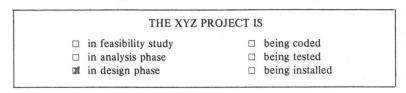

THE XYZ PROJECT IS

☐ in feasibility study   ☐ being coded
☐ in analysis phase   ☐ being tested
☑ in design phase   ☐ being installed

Figure 3.3. An inferior way to track a project.

There are real-world pressures to operate several life cycle phases in parallel. For example, if the users want fast results and if management agrees that quick results are necessary, perhaps you should begin the design phase before analysis is 100 percent complete. Or, say you have a fixed project team of two systems analysts, two design specialists, and five coders. What are you going to do with the coders during the analysis and design phases? The only logical answer is to have them start preliminary coding.

In another case, assume that, during the coding phase, you discover an error made during analysis. Remembering the dire warnings sounded earlier in this chapter, you decide to go back to the analysis phase to fix the error. Must you stop all coding, or can you operate the phases in parallel? Or, the user demands that certain key functions of the new system be made available as soon as possible. He won't wait for the entire system to be completed to get the key functions. How are you going to do it? A realistic view of systems development, then, must take into account the need to revert to earlier phases as necessary and to operate various phases in parallel (see Figure 3.4).

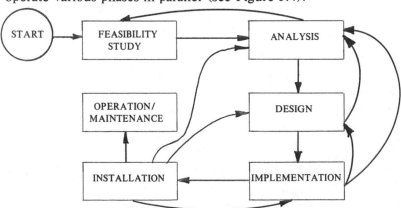

Figure 3.4. An alternate systems development life cycle.

3.1 A flexible approach to systems development

Structured or radical development permits the developer to meet the requirements of overlap, feedback, and flexibility. As stated earlier, the term often used for the traditional life cycle is conservative development, which holds that a given phase should be essentially complete before the next phase begins. The term used for the flexible technique is radical development, which holds that the various phases can successfully occur in parallel.

In *Managing the Structured Techniques,* Ed Yourdon gives an example of how advocates of both conservative and radical development would perform top-down design and coding of a system, and some of the reasons for choosing one or the other.

> We could describe the radical top-down approach in the following manner: First, design the top level of a system — that is, recognize that [a] payroll system . . . will have a top-level edit module, a top-level update module, and a variety of top-level print modules. Having done this much design, *immediately* write the code for these modules, and test them as a Version 1 system. Next, design the second-level modules, those modules a level below the top-level modules just completed. Having designed the second-level modules, next write the code and test a Version 2 system, and so forth.
>
> The conservative approach to top-down implementation consists of designing all the top-level modules, then the next level, then all third-level modules, and so on until the entire design is finished. Then code the top-level modules and implement them as Version 1. From the experience gained in implementing Version 1, make any necessary changes to the lower levels of design, then code and test at the second level, and on down to the lowest level.
>
> The important thing to realize is that the radical approach and the conservative approach represent the two extreme points on a spectrum. There are an infinite number of compromise top-down strategies that you can select, depending on your situation. You may decide, for example, to finish 75 percent of the design, and then begin coding and testing those modules that you have designed. (Obviously, the coding and testing would be done top-down.) Or you might decide to design 25 percent of the system — and then, with 75 percent of the system still fuzzy, start coding and implementing.*

You can imagine the same approach being taken during the analysis phase, with believers in the conservative method fully laying out the data flow diagrams (DFDs), data dictionary (DD), and mini-

---

*E. Yourdon, *Managing the Structured Techniques,* 2nd ed. (New York: Yourdon Press, 1979), pp. 74-75. Reprinted by permission.

specifications — probably for both the current and new systems in both their physical and logical forms — for the entire system before proceeding to design.

The radical approach, on the other hand, might well begin design as soon as two or three levels of DFDs and DD definitions are prepared. (The minispecs might only be partially documented, even when using a tool like structured English.)

Which approach should you choose? Here's Yourdon's view:

> As you may have guessed, there is no single right answer. I cannot tell you whether the radical approach is better than the conservative approach for all possible projects. However, I *can* identify the primary factors that will help *you* decide just how radical or conservative you will want to be:
>
> • *User fickleness.* If the user has no idea of what he wants, or has a tendency to change his mind, I would opt for the radical approach. Why waste time designing a great deal of detailed logic that will be thrown away? On the other hand, if the user knows precisely what he wants, I might attempt a complete design.
>
> • *Design quality.* Committing oneself to code too early in the project may make it difficult to improve the design later. All other things being equal, we prefer to finish the entire design.
>
> • *Time pressures.* If you are under extreme pressure from users or higher levels of management to produce some tangible output quickly, go for the radical approach. If your deadline is absolutely inflexible, i.e., if it is a case of "you bet your job," go for the radical approach. If you are not under much pressure, and if the deadline is flexible, go for the conservative approach.
>
> • *Accurate estimates.* If you are required by your organization to provide accurate, detailed estimates of schedules, manpower, and other resources, then you should opt for the conservative approach. How can you estimate how long it will take to implement the system until you know how many modules it will contain?*

There is no exhaustive and generally accepted list of pros and cons for the radical and conservative approaches. There are, however, some generally agreed upon points, which are given in the following subsections.

---

*Ibid., p. 75. Reprinted by permission.

3.1.1 Advantages of the conservative approach

The first benefit of conservative development is that *the activities are well defined and well understood.* Everyone knows exactly what is going on at a given time. When an activity — say, analysis — is done, it's done. Further, we can define the activity using a straightforward checklist, and can conveniently track project progress using a simple "you are here" technique.

Second, *conservative development is comfortable for management.* The "you are here" concept makes it easy for managers — particularly non-data-processing managers (like users) — to understand where the project is at any given moment. I think this comfort comes from the innate feeling that if there is only one thing going on at a time, a person can keep track of the project *even if he or she doesn't really understand it.* (Consider, as a non-data-processing analogy, the relative complexity of managing — or even of watching — a three-ring American-style circus versus a one-ring European-style circus.)

Third, *the conservative approach provides clear go/no-go checkpoints.* Because no phase in a fully conservative project can begin until completion of phase-end formalities, this approach assures neat end points at which an audit can be conducted.

Conservative development is safer if turnover is anticipated. Because conservative development takes place step by step and is easy to control and review, it is easier to assure that every task is completed and fully documented before another task begins. Therefore, if someone leaves the project, it will be comparatively easier for someone else to pick up the work.

Systems built in this way have fewer errors. If you plan everything in advance (that is, if you plan the shape of the entire design before beginning design, and the entire set of modules before coding any of them), you won't experience many development problems that result from a lack of planning. For example, the interfaces between various systems and modules will be explicitly stated in advance, and should be less likely to cause problems.

Conservative development enables control over changes. Because of the ability to set up checkpoints easily, you can insure comprehensive documentation at every stage of the project; and as a result, can insure that the documentation is modified as necessary to keep it up-to-date.

Finally, *conservative development allows use of commercially available systems development life cycle methodologies and of so-called project management packages.* This is true because, for the most part, the various methodologies and packages do assume that a conservative strategy will be used.

3.1.2 Advantages of the radical approach

Radical development provides for early payback through earlier installation of certain system functions. Frequently, certain functions to be provided by a new system can be identified as being critical to the user. A radical approach can move those functions through the systems development life cycle quickly to produce an operational subset of the final system containing those key functions. Later, subsequent releases, which will have more functions, will be implemented. These later releases represent *supersets* of the original release. While these upgrades are in preparation, the users are already gaining the benefits of the key functions.

Radical development provides for early evaluation of interfaces. My experience, as well as that of many of my colleagues, indicates that systems tend to break down at their points of interface. The breakdown can be at the interface between modules, between subsystems, between systems (for instance, general ledger transactions or journal entries passed to accounting systems), between the system and its files, or between the system and the outside world. Because radical development gets an initial version of the system up and running quickly, it provides for early exercising — and thus testing and evaluation — of these potential problem areas of the system.

Radical development allows for the use of prototyping tools. Many systems development departments are making use of so-called nonprocedural languages to quickly implement initial test versions of systems. Clearly, this differs from the top-down concept of implementing various releases and versions of systems by using subsets of the actual final code. But the idea of showing a working piece of the system to the user and of letting the user try it out to solidify final requirements is right in line with the ideas of radical development.

Radical development speeds up the division of big problems into smaller, more manageable problems. The simple concept underlying structured systems development is that big problems can be broken into smaller and smaller problems through the process of functional decomposition. If you can solve the small problems and if you understand the interfaces between them, then you've solved the big problem. Radical development forces you to concentrate on decomposition right from the start in order to have portions of the system ready for design and coding at the earliest opportunity. This emphasis on partitioning the problem accelerates understanding of the system and the problems involved in building it.

Radical development leads to improved staff morale. I've heard many systems development managers comment that their staff members enjoy working on radical development projects. "People can see things happening," they say. The managers point out that workers can lose intensity during a long project. Vitality can be drained by the seemingly endless analysis and design phases of long-term, conservative development projects. Radical development, which results in versions of the system being brought into operation and turned over to users, helps keep everyone focused on the actual problem, making them feel part of a real, live, successful systems development process.

Radical development leads to effective use of human resources. Put yourself in the place of the project manager who, on the first day of a three-year project, is given a fixed staff of three analysts, two design specialists, one database specialist, two procedure writers, one project secretary/librarian, and ten coders. What are you going to do with the coders? In a conservative project, that could represent a problem. It could be months before anything is ready for coding. There is, consequently, an understandable tendency to create make-work projects, such as "develop a general-purpose error handling routine" or "develop a general-purpose input editing routine." In the radical development environment, by contrast, there is meaningful work for everyone very quickly. Certainly, if variable staffing is available to the manager of a conservative project, this problem can be minimized. But in many organizations, variable staffing is simply not an option.

3.1.3 Disadvantages of the conservative approach

Clearly, you can turn around most of the advantages of the radical approach and present them as disadvantages of the conservative approach, so I won't repeat all of them. But let's look at three that do appear to be significant:

The conservative approach does not build morale. As I have pointed out before (and undoubtedly will again), a lot of data processing people can go far in their careers without ever implementing a system. By transferring to various projects within an organization, or by well-timed moves from company to company, they can manage to avoid the nitty gritty work of installing a system. They also manage to avoid blame for large failures (even though they may have done an inadequate analysis job and deserve the blame).

Conservative development leads to building obsolete systems. In conservative projects, there is a tendency to avoid re-entering an already completed phase to redo work as required by continuing changes in user requirements. Such changes are considered "enhancements" to be handled as system updates following implementation. As a result, you may well be implementing a system with known deficiencies, which could have been remedied during systems development. I consider these unfixed problems to be evidence of obsolescence! Management never likes to hear that it just spent a huge sum of money to develop a system that will have to be repaired almost immediately or redone in order to work properly.

Conservative systems tend to be implemented all at once. This criticism goes to the heart of the argument that large systems ought to be implemented in stages (called releases), so that key functions are available to users as early as possible. Users often don't know exactly what they want in the total system, and radical development provides flexibility to meet the users' uncertainty. There is also the real problem of the users' capacity to absorb the changes that accompany new systems. Many specialists in system installation call for phased implementation to spread the installation effort over a longer time period, thus reducing the speed of change. They call for *evolutionary* installation, as opposed to sudden, dislocating *revolutionary installation.*

3.1.4 Disadvantages of the radical approach

Unfortunately, in their zeal to implement new and better systems development techniques, developers often fail to critically review the new techniques — as in the case of those who unquestioningly adopt radical systems development as gospel — and to understand their shortcomings. In the following paragraphs, I discuss four valid criticisms of the radical approach. Be warned that failure to understand the potential problems can lead to disaster.

Radical development may delay the installation of the total system and increase its eventual cost. Some managers argue that conservative development leads to the planned and orderly installation of a system. They charge that radical development, with its multiple versions of the system and installations, requires the duplication of at least some effort and thus increases the total project development time. They also point out that the multiple training periods for users and the interim procedures that must be developed to support the various versions can increase overall project cost. Further, they state that radical development provides the user with too many opportunities to change the system under development, thus increasing the cost and delaying final implementation of the new system.

Radical development provides poor visibility of total project cost. Critics of radical development charge that because of the fluid nature of the project, with various phases and releases of the system in different stages of development, management can't easily determine the total cost of the final, delivered, fully operational system. (Of course, one could argue that it is better to admit to a degree of uncertainty of costs for future releases than to risk embarrassment by guessing total costs during the feasibility survey.)

Radically managed projects may never get done. What if the users decide that some intermediate release is good enough? They might feel that the capabilities implemented, say, in Version 2 are all that they need, and cancel the rest of the project. You never get to put in all of the bells and whistles planned for the final release. Disaster, right? Probably not. After all, the purpose of systems development projects is to satisfy user requirements in a cost-effective way, *not* to build monuments to the DP department's technical magnificence. If you've truly followed the principles of top-down development, whatever release the user decides is the one he wants will be a complete, well-documented, and (ideally) well-controlled system. If you've solved the user's problem at a lower cost than either you or he expected, that's all to the good. Of course, there is a case in which user fixation on a non-final version of the system could be a problem, as when you've been using a non-procedural tool to put up a quick-and-dirty prototype of a system. While the prototype building tools in radical development provide for fast development, they tend to use machine resources in a dreadfully inefficient way. Failure to replace the prototype with more efficient code could result in a significant waste of DP resources if the prototype were used for a long time. This is as much a political problem as a technical one, and can be prevented by good communication with the user *before* the project starts. The user should understand that the prototype system must be replaced with an efficient system.

Radical development leads to a lack of conceptual integrity or architectural consistency. This argument warns that, unless care is taken, a system designed under a radical strategy can look like an uncoordinated committee effort. Various parts of the system may be designed quite differently. To avoid chaos, the project manager needs to impose some degree of standardization, so that the final system has a consistent internal architecture.

3.2 Problems in auditing radically developed systems

With the new model of structured systems development and without the traditional end-phase checkpoints, several key problems regarding audits must be considered by the project manager, auditor, users, and senior management:

- When will there be quality assurance sign-offs for each phase?

- How can there be effective audit reviews if the signed-off product is subject to change?

- How can effective internal controls be assured in a radical environment?

- When can management make its go/no-go decisions?

In short, if we weaken the boundaries between life cycle phases, how will we know where we are at any given moment (as we presumably do in Figure 3.1)? To address these questions, let's start with some ground rules that are not subject to much argument:

Rule: Radical development is no excuse for poor controls.

All systems have to include appropriate internal controls, regardless of how they are developed, as stated in Chapter 1.

Rule: The need for managerial control over the systems development effort is independent of the development strategy employed.

It is unrealistic to assume that either data processing managers or users will accept having less control over the development project because radical techniques are in use.

Rule: The EDP auditor's responsibilities during systems development are also independent of the development strategy.

Systems developed using the radical approach must be subject to the same level of review as systems developed using the conservative approach.

From these rules, we see that we must subject radically developed systems to the same degree of control and of management review as we do a more traditionally developed system. But how? The need for logical review points in radical systems development is just as real as in the conservative approach. The only difference is that the review points aren't quite as obvious. The end points of traditional development phases (which have long served as the review points by users, DP managers, and auditors) are clear to all. Such points as "end of analysis" or "end of design" cry out for sign-offs and other various DP rites of passage.

To control radical development, we can borrow a concept from structured analysis: We can divide the traditional big review and sign-off session into a collection of smaller reviews of limited scope. Each of the major functions of systems development (such as analysis and

nts of the
he *solution*
al design,
agram, or
a system
large, one
design —
gn, of the
e recovery
rocedural''
f the logic
sign would
dule.

ganizations
he product
g. Unfor-
   problems
ughs were
who spent

of the test
e test run.
erson who
luding the
aps a user

you are to suc-
stems develop-

*s. Modi-
valuation
reviewers
product
producer

d *not* be

n Press,

---

he most radical of projects, but just
once. In order to establish mini-
of work that pass from phase to
level bubble that is to be decom-
subnetwork* resulting in structure
of coding, the basic unit of work is

end traditional review with a collec-
advantages: First, since the mini-
the system, it is easier to evaluate
the controls. Second, since the re-
d occur earlier in the development
iciencies found should be less. Fi-
n scope and the increased ease of
reviews, much of the work can be
systems development personnel,
ional auditing or quality assurance

the evaluation of control in mini-
the walkthrough process. Walk-
chniques that help improve the
eviewed. Isn't appropriate control

en assume that walkthroughs are
g could be further from the truth.
walkthroughs at every stage of the
he following examples show:

he name implies, a review of the
fications, of a computer system.
es a systems analyst, a user
esigners; its primary purpose is to
biguities, and omissions in the
is reviewed in the walkthrough
the proposed system, a flowchart,
ary, or any other suitable descrip-
tem.

hat will be implemented as a unit.
input to the design process from

Design walkthroughs assume that the functional requirem
system have been correctly stated and emphasize instead
to the problem. There may be walkthroughs of a log
usually documented with a data flow diagram, HIPO c
structure chart; or of a physical design, documented wit
flowchart or other appropriate document. If a system is
can find walkthroughs of different aspects of the physica
for instance, separate walkthroughs of the database des
design of the telecommunications subsystem, and of tl
subsystem. Also, there may be a walkthrough of a "
design — that is, the low-level flowchart or pseudocode
within individual modules. The performing of such a de
immediately precede the actual writing of code for the me

Code walkthroughs often attract the most attention in or
— simply because they have never been done before. 1
being reviewed is, obviously, the code — a program listi
tunately, code walkthroughs sometimes uncover analys
or design problems (usually because preceding walkthr
ignored or superficial) to the dismay of the programme
days writing brilliant code.

Test walkthroughs are conducted to insure the adequacy
data for the system — *not* to examine the output from t
Attendees at such a walkthrough typically include the
developed the test data, other programmers (probably ir
author of the program*), a systems analyst, and per
representative if he can be enticed to join the fun.[†]

There are three requirements that must be met if
cessfully use walkthroughs to monitor controls in the sy
ment life cycle:

- *Make control part of your walkthrough standar*
  fy the rules for walkthroughs to make the
  of internal control a part of the review. The
  should consider the need for control in th
  under review, and determine how and if the
  has achieved that control.

---

*Note the strong implication here that the author of the program sho
the one who develops the test data.
[†]E. Yourdon, *Structured Walkthroughs,* 2nd ed. (New York: Yourd
1978), pp. 18-19. Reprinted by permission.

- *Make sure all attendees know the principles of good control.* Clearly, if any walkthrough is to be useful, the reviewers must have sufficient technical competence to review the product. For example, it makes little sense to assign the review of an assembly language module to a group having no knowledge of assembly language. The rule is simple: If you don't know what constitutes rightness, how are you going to recognize wrongness?

  Some years ago, I performed an EDP audit for the New York City branch of a major European bank, which ran a COBOL shop. Everything went fine until I was ready to review the documentation and samples of the code. Since I was a fair-to-middling COBOL programmer, I figured I was all set. I was wrong. The documentation *looked* great, but it was written in German, and the programs were written in German COBOL.

  The point is that to be effective walkthrough reviewers of control, the systems developers of course must be technically proficient, but they must also learn about what constitutes control. This book provides a reference guide. Formal training in internal control helps, too, but there's no substitute for on-the-job training. Have internal auditors or quality assurance people work with you, either as advisors, teachers, or walkthrough attendees, and you're on your way.

- *Follow up to be sure that control is being evaluated during the walkthroughs.* Practice a bit of quality assurance on your quality assurance efforts. Many project management specialists have suggested that you track program problems to determine the effectiveness of walkthroughs. Similarly, I'm suggesting that you track control weaknesses detected in applications by people external to the design team (such as auditors, users, quality assurance specialists) to determine whether certain types of problems are not being detected by project team members. If so, you can take remedial action to improve control evaluation during the walkthrough process.

3.2.1 The auditing/quality assurance role

If we make control reviews part of the ongoing walkthrough process, aren't we eliminating the role of the EDP auditor or quality assurance specialist? Quite the contrary. I maintain that by placing primary responsibility for good control in the hands of the project team, we free the internal control specialists to do the job that they are being paid to do.

If specialists are forced to spend all of their time looking at the nitty gritty details of control throughout a system, there is little or (too often) no time remaining to consider the organization's overall need for control, or even to consider major applications taken in their entirety. Indeed, with the limited auditing and quality assurance resources available in today's organizations, it is tragic to force a decision between reviewing the trees (the individual control points) and the forest (the overall control of the system). Yet this is done every day. Is it not better to separate the duty of watching the trees from that of managing the forest as a whole?

The auditor who is faced with the review of a radical type of project can easily be swamped by the work volume. But if the detailed reviews are performed in the course of walkthroughs, the auditor can spend his time sampling to determine the effectiveness of the walkthrough reviews, examining the overall structure of controls, and handling the arbitration of auditing questions that have arisen. The auditor or quality assurance specialist is free to act as an *advisor* and as a *consultant* on controls. In short, by giving the day-to-day responsibility for control reviews to the project team, the auditor or quality assurance specialist regains some of the independence so necessary for the proper performance of his duties. Because more people pay closer attention to controls, the organization ends up with better systems.

3.3 Summary

In this chapter, I've shown that many project management and project auditing concepts are founded on a fairy tale: They are based on sequential execution of life cycle phases with neat sign-offs following each phase as a prerequisite for beginning work on the next phase. But we've also seen that a model for systems development that assumes purely sequential execution of phases, without iteration or feedback, is not realistic. Regardless of the system being developed and the organization doing the work, developers will sometimes have to return to earlier phases to correct errors or to accommodate user changes in requirements. And because of time pressures, it may pay to allow parallel development of various phases.

The range of choices for development methodologies extend from ultra-radical to ultra-conservative development. There are significant advantages and disadvantages associated with each approach. One major problem concerns the difficulty of auditing radically developed projects because of their non-linear process. As suggested, a well-thought-out plan for walkthroughs throughout the systems development process should be implemented to review the system's controls. However, walkthroughs are not to serve as a vehicle for building controls into the systems; rather, controls must be designed and built as part of the systems development process. How that can be done in the structured development environment is the subject of the following chapters.

4 | Application Controls: An Introduction

Internal controls implement the user policy regarding the accuracy, completeness, and security of an application system. Of course, this conceptual definition by itself is not enough to enable us to build controls into a real-life system. We also need an operational definition of the internal controls of applications — that is, a definition of each type of control and the circumstances under which it is required. The second part of this chapter provides you with this definition by giving you a tool for analyzing what controls a system has and what controls it needs. The first part of this chapter clarifies what an internal control does by defining accuracy, completeness, and security and by examining the role of controls in insuring them.

A warning: In this book, I'm considering controls over applications, *not* controls over the systems development process. While they go hand-in-hand, they are different. If you want more information on the controls over the development process, I refer you to books on the management of structured systems development projects.*

Since users and systems developers don't often actively consider controls in new systems and since one of our avowed purposes is a bit of consciousness raising, I begin this chapter with a small melodrama. I hope it keeps you in suspense while you cheer the hero and boo the villains (if you can identify them). I also hope that this scenario won't appear to be taken from your own shop, but it just might.

---

*Specifically, I recommend these three books: Thomas R. Gildersleeve's *Data Processing Project Management* (New York: Van Nostrand Reinhold, 1974); Brian Dickinson's *Developing Structured Systems: A Methodology Using Structured Techniques* (New York: Yourdon Press, 1980); and Ed Yourdon's *Managing the System Life Cycle* (New York: Yourdon Press, 1982).

4.1 Mission unlikely: a melodrama

It was a miracle! Never in all my years had I received an audit report like that received by our accounts payable system. The joint team of internal and external auditors *loved it,* and reported that the system worked well and had excellent internal controls. So our course of action was charted, our objective clear: We would do to all other systems whatever we had done to the accounts payable system.

"Assemble the team that built the accounts payable system, and hustle them in here," I ordered. After a few minutes, my assistant returned to say, "Sorry, boss, no can do. They've passed on."

"Tragic," I said, "to die so young, with so many systems projects still before them; bless their control-oriented hearts."

"They aren't dead — they've simply gone to other companies," my assistant replied.

"Confound those disloyal DPers. But not to worry. I've got an alternate plan." I unlocked my desk safe and removed a business card. It contained only a number. I dialed it.

Two days later, Sheerluck Jones, the world's greatest DP detective, arrived. "Sheerluck, we need your not inconsiderable talents to find the internal controls in the accounts payable system and show them to us, so that we can teach others to build well-controlled systems," I directed.

Suitably enthroned in a borrowed office, Sheerluck soon issued his first orders: "Get me the programs. I'll knock this project off by lunch time."

Three days later, the office overflowed with listings. "I've read every line on every page, and I didn't find any controls, just COBOL and Job Control Language statements. The answer undoubtedly lies in the program specs. Send them to me in the conference room. I'm moving to larger quarters." He searched the pseudocode day and night, but found nothing. For several more days and nights, he searched the structure charts, and then moved on to the system specifications. Still nothing.

Winter turned into spring, and finally Sheerluck emerged. "I found data flow diagrams, a data dictionary, minispecs, and some data structure diagrams. But nothing labeled controls. I have a plan to kidnap those former employees who developed the system. Once I get them into my hands, I have ways of making them talk!"

Before I could give his unusual — but possibly necessary — proposal much consideration, a note came from the head of our internal audit function. Since we had never had Sheerluck's contract approved by the finance department (true, but expedient), the manager ordered his contract terminated forthwith. Then, I noticed a comment penciled at the bottom of the manager's letter: *Controls are user requirements. Nothing more, nothing less.*

That's it! No wonder Sheerluck couldn't find them. He assumed they were different from everything else in the system, that they would stand out like the proverbial sore thumb. When he couldn't find them, he believed that they had been cleverly hidden. But we were wrong. Controls *aren't different;* they are a part of the solution to the user's problem and just mingle in with all the other systems requirements.

4.2 What are application controls?

Our definition of internal controls in an application tells us that they are responses to user requirements for the accuracy, completeness, and security of information systems. Let's look at each of these requirements in more detail.

4.2.1 Accuracy

At first glance, accuracy does not seem to be an issue. Who wants an inaccurate system? No one, of course, but accuracy is relative. And assurance of accuracy always costs you, either in dollars, efficiency, or ease of use. For example, the *existence* of a check digit on an account number is not an effective control measure. It is the *checking* of the check digit that is the control. The check digit test should probably be carried out every time the number is entered into the system. But every time the computer executes a check digit test, it must take the time to calculate the check digit and compare it to the input check digit. Admittedly, this task takes nanoseconds or, perhaps, microseconds, but consider how that can add up in the case of a credit card processor handling tens of millions of transactions a month. Or, consider the problem of assuring the accuracy of data communications: The more redundancy built into the system, the more accurate the system becomes, yet the more it costs and, often, the less efficient it becomes.

There are many other issues concerning accuracy, including how to treat rounding errors, and how to establish a cost-effective level of accuracy. For example, in interest calculations, how should the system handle rounding? There have been reported in the press a number of so-called salami swindles in which perpetrators round down bank accounts or stock share prices by fractions of cents, and place the amount taken off in an account to which they have access. By accumulating the "breakage" of huge numbers of accounts or shares, such accounts can amass hundreds of thousands of dollars.

Various controls and edits inform us of errors, but can we afford to investigate all of them? Probably not. We have to take the position that what we are looking for is some *cost-effective level of accuracy*. Just what this level is depends on many things, including the value and sensitivity of the data, the effects of errors, and management's willingness to pay to avoid errors. Remember that expenditures to improve accuracy follow a diminishing returns curve: The first expenditures bring great increase in accuracy; added expenditures bring less per dollar spent, because systems developers generally have to use more sophisticated techniques to find more and more errors, and because, as developers strive for greater accuracy, they become concerned with lower-frequency errors.

So, while no one doubts the need for accuracy, there are questions about how much accuracy is required, how much everyone involved is willing to pay for accuracy, and how much complexity the user is willing to accept to insure accuracy. Clearly, these are management issues, but they also must be understood — and the eventual decisions implemented — by systems developers and by internal control specialists.

4.2.2 Completeness

Completeness might seem to be the same thing as accuracy, but there are some significant differences. Completeness means processing everything that is supposed to be processed, whereas accuracy means processing a transaction correctly. One can exist without the other.

When we talk of completeness, we mean assuring that all transactions (or all records, or all of whatever is appropriate) are presented to a system for processing. Consider a clerk who is manually entering a batch of 25 transactions into a computer. As each is entered, it is processed. Let's assume that the clerk sneezes, and that the force of that prodigious sneeze blows one of the transactions off the desk. Let's also assume that the clerk doesn't notice. If the computer perfectly processes the 24 transactions that were entered, will the reports based on those transactions be accurate? (Now, what I'm about to tell you is a matter of semantics, but bear with me.)

The reports are accurate *as far as they go*, but they aren't complete. So at the bottom line, the report that requires all 25 transactions is unusable (that is, wrong). "Wrong is wrong," you may say. But there are all kinds of wrongness. There can be significant differences between what I'd consider "wrong" and what someone else would call "wrong," just as there are differences in, say, "snow." To me, snow is snow, but to skiers, snow may be "corn," "powder," or "granular."

If you are concerned with internal control either as a user, systems developer, or auditor, the difference between accuracy and completeness should be significant to you because each requires different kinds of controls. Understanding the differences leads to conscious consideration of *both* controls to guarantee accuracy and controls to guarantee completeness.

4.2.3 Security

There are as many definitions of security as there are people defining it. I like the one that defines security as *those measures that are taken to protect information from accidental or intentional (but unauthorized) destruction, modification, or compromise.* Let's take a closer look at the definition.

A security breach can be either accidental or intentional. The vast majority of security problems are traced to errors or omissions by employees doing their regular jobs. Deliberate acts by disgruntled employees or outsiders are rare. Yet, too many systems developers suffer from what I call the James Bond syndrome; that is, they act as if their installations are going to be attacked by some evil organization. These people install all sorts of sophisticated physical safeguards around their computer centers. Tens of millions of dollars are spent for card-type locks, sophisticated surveillance systems, encryption devices, and exotic fire extinguishing gasses. These are necessary in proper measure, but they cover only a small part of the risk. The odds are good that if a problem occurs, an innocent mistake will have caused it.

Security specialists teach us that there are three harmful things that can happen to data: It can be destroyed, modified, or compromised. In the first case (destruction of data), tapes can be damaged or erased. Disks can be overwritten. If misaligned by a few thousandths of an inch, disks will suffer head crashes, which are often fatal to the data. These problems can be prevented by controls to assure that the right files are used, that there is suitable backup, and that the destruction of obsolete files is carried out under proper control.

Second, modifying files without proper authorization can be more dangerous than destroying the files. When files have been destroyed, at least you know you've got trouble. If they have only been altered, the problem may be hidden for a period. During that time, managers may be basing decisions on wrong information. Controls to assure that there has been no unauthorized modification are vital if a system is to be usable.

Third is the problem of who has access to the data. Who may see what information from which files? Competitors who obtain financial or operational data may do serious harm. Whenever data concerns people, the problem of protecting privacy arises. In some cases, legal or regulatory restrictions should control release of personal, financial, or medical data about employees or customers. Privacy is an active interest of the consumer movement.

In sum, assuring cost-effective controls in our systems is a high priority for systems developers. In the next section, I give you a tool that will allow you to assess methodically the need for controls in the systems you build and maintain.*

4.3 Identifying and understanding internal controls

Probably the most difficult problem facing the systems analyst or inexperienced auditor is how to identify controls efficiently in an existing system or in a system that is under development. The best way is to use an analysis tool. The rest of this chapter describes one such tool that I've used with success. This tool is a decision tree whose branches consist of categories and questions that guide you toward the controls on the end branches. It can be used on any system you have under development, whether you use the methods of this book or not. I choose to use this decision tree as the analysis tool for three reasons: First, it forces you to break the system, at least conceptually, into chunks. Second, where appropriate, it poses some control-related questions that you must answer before proceeding. Finally, it offers alternative controls according to how you answered the questions.

The decision tree is to be used at different points during systems analysis, as explained in Chapter 6. When used as a tool to analyze an existing system, the decision tree enables you to see how controls are implemented and to identify weaknesses in control. When used as a tool for developing controls in a new system, it challenges the analyst to answer a series of questions that lead to suggestions for controls. But they are only suggestions; no tool can give definitive solutions for all systems.

On the following pages, I show and discuss the major branches of the control analysis decision tree.

---

*This outline of internal controls is derived from the American Institute of Certified Public Accountants Audit and Accounting Guide, *The Auditors Study and Evaluation of Internal Control in EDP Systems,* copyright © 1977 American Institute of CPAs, New York, New York. Used by permission. The outline originated when institute members faced the problem of teaching accountants how to review clients' systems. They reasoned that if they could understand the kinds of controls available, they would have in effect a shopping list of controls to consider for use during systems development.

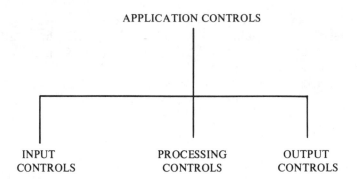

Figure 4.1. The three major classes of application controls.

It is traditional to divide consideration of controls into one of three classes, as shown in Figure 4.1: controls over inputs, controls over processing, and controls over outputs.

4.4 Input controls

We begin the analysis of controls by considering the controls over inputs of a system. These controls are the most important and the most numerous, as most errors are generated by input processing. Throughout this discussion, remember that, whenever we speak of a "system," we should avoid limiting our consideration to automated portions of a system. We must look at the *entire* system, or all of our work will be in vain.

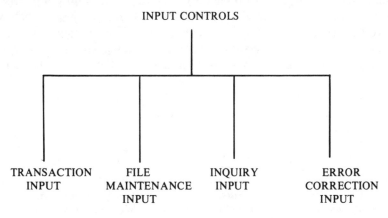

Figure 4.2. Types of input controls.

Figure 4.2 indicates that before we can properly consider the control requirements of input data streams, we must first realize that various inputs perform different functions in systems. These different functions may call for different controls. For example, an input that consists of requests for information from a file may require less control than an input that orders the system to permanently erase or alter the contents of a file. These differences mean that you must assign every input stream in the system to one of the following four major categories: transactions, file maintenance, inquiries, and error corrections. In the case of a physical data stream that contains multiple types of inputs, we want to separate the various types of inputs, even if they physically come from the same place and are intermingled. Each of these categories is briefly described below.

Transaction inputs are the normal everyday work flows of the system; they usually result in records being modified, added, deleted, or updated. To differentiate them from other input streams, consider that transaction inputs are usually generated by activities performed every day. For example, in an airline reservation system, a request to reserve or cancel space is a transaction input.

File maintenance inputs, like transaction inputs, cause files to be updated. Unlike transaction streams, they are *not* usually generated by routine, everyday activities, and the files that are changed are typically the files that are used to either process or direct the processing of transactions. These inputs can be readily differentiated from normal transaction flows. For example, in our airline reservation system, changes in the scheduling of flights, or in the listing of aircraft to be used for specific flights, are file maintenance inputs. Similarly, inputs that are used to maintain various edit tables are file maintenance inputs. As you can imagine, maintenance inputs are critical to an organization. For example, if incorrect file maintenance was performed on the flight reservations file, the reservation agents might be unaware of an actual flight that was omitted from the file. Being unaware of it, the reservation agents couldn't sell tickets for the flight, and a substantial revenue loss would result.

Inquiry inputs are inputs that request information from a system, but that do not change the records of the system. For example, a request for a flight schedule or for a depositor's status doesn't affect the information stored. Although these inputs may offer less possibility of damaging the system than inputs that alter the file, they cannot be ignored when control is considered. We may want to verify that requests are authorized and to record access to the information, or restrict certain users to limited subsets of the available information. As with maintenance inputs, it is usually easy to identify a system's inquiry input streams.

By *error correction inputs,* I mean inputs to fix blunders: not the day-to-day re-entry of transactions that are rejected by a system, but the rare direct manipulation of file contents to correct a disastrous error. For example, what if we discovered that through a previously undetected program error, our corporate general ledger has gone out of balance? Somehow, a debit was entered in the file without a corresponding credit. How are we going to bring the file back into synchronization, given that a one-sided entry (that is, debit-only or credit-only) entry is not valid? There are two general ways in which the problem is usually handled: In one case, the systems developers have developed a transaction to permit a normally forbidden transaction to be processed under stringent safeguards; in the second case, a utility program is used to directly modify the contents of the master file. In either case, error correction inputs need extensive controls to avoid unauthorized or improper use.

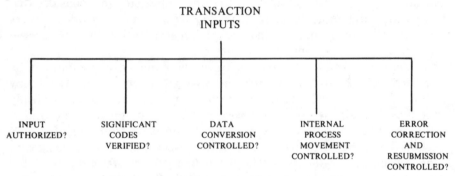

Figure 4.3. Major input control questions.

The control requirements of each input stream can now be evaluated. To assist in the evaluation, five questions should be addressed, as illustrated in Figure 4.3. The answer to each question must take into account the potential risk if errors are made and not detected, the probability of problems occurring, and the cost of controls in both money and complexity. If you carefully answer the five questions, you will have performed a thorough evaluation of the need for control over the particular input.

- *Is this input authorized?* How do you know that the transaction is supposed to be entered? How do you know that the person who entered it is authorized to do so?

- *Are significant codes verified?* Should certain fields on the input be evaluated for accuracy?

- *Is data conversion properly controlled?* When an input stream has to be converted from one form to another (paper to electronic image, for example), how do you know that the information that goes into the conversion process is the same as that which emerges?

- *Is internal process movement controlled?* When the input is subjected to several processing steps, how do you know that nothing is added or deleted during the process between the steps?

- *Are the correction of errors and the resubmission of corrected transactions controlled?* In many applications, there are specific rules concerning the re-entry of rejected transactions. What are those rules for your application, and what controls are in place to enforce them?

We will look at each question in more detail in the following sections.

4.4.1 Is this input authorized?

Figure 4.4 indicates that there are four general ways to determine whether transactions are authorized. Depending on circumstances, these may be used singly or in combination.

A *pre-processing test* is a manual test employed before processing the transactions to determine whether we should, in fact, permit them to be processed. For example, we can review the inputs to determine whether they bear the signature of a person authorized to approve them.

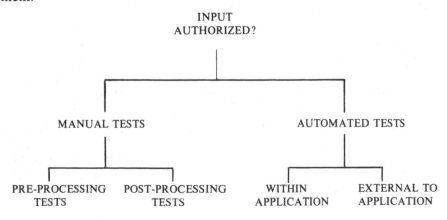

Figure 4.4. Input authorization tests.

A *post-processing test* is a manual test performed *after* processing the transactions to determine whether they should have been processed. For example, if a department reviews a transaction log and matches it to authorized transactions, the test could identify any inputs that had been processed, but not authorized. In this event, of course, any unauthorized transactions must be backed out. The timing of the post-review process must be carefully considered. For example, if we were reviewing payroll change transactions, we would probably want to review them before we permitted the new information to be used to produce checks.

Post-processing tests are frequently used when quick processing of an input stream is desired, and when a low rate of rejects is expected. A good example is that of check clearance between banks. All checks are assumed to be good and paid. Only later, when a small percentage are found to be unpayable (for insufficient funds or other reasons), are they returned and the payment reclaimed.

For an *automated test within an application,* the computer is programmed to determine whether the input is authorized (for example, by checking a special list or a transaction-specific password).

For an *automated test external to an application,* authorization decisions are delegated to a program external to the application. For example, a security system may check the password and authority tables for a user to assure that only authorized users have access to the system.

You can see how tests might be combined. For example, we might restrict the right to enter payroll change transactions to a limited number of users, and use a security pre-processor, external to the application, to determine if an authorized user is on the line. But we might also want a manual post-processing test to be certain that all of the transactions entered are supported by authorized hard-copy transactions.

4.4.2 Are significant codes verified?

There are three different ways to verify the accuracy of the significant codes in input streams: check sum tests, internal consistency tests, and validity tests, as shown in Figure 4.5.

Check sum tests: Check digits can be used to review the accuracy of specific fields. For example, a check digit can help determine whether an account number is valid. (Note that this is *very* different from saying that the number you have is the *right* number. You can have the wrong valid number, and the check digit test will never reveal it.) Remember that the check digit test is different from the check digit. Just having a check digit associated with a number doesn't help you at all! You must also perform the test.

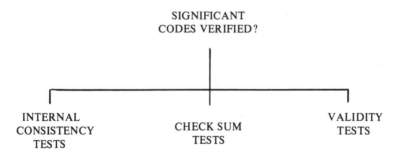

Figure 4.5. Tests to verify significant codes.

Internal consistency tests: In some applications, it may be possible to verify accuracy by comparing the values of various fields to determine whether the combinations make sense. For example, if a medical record contains a valid test type, "Pap Smear," in the field representing "Type of Test" and also indicates that the sex of the patient is "M," there is a problem. Similarly, if the "Country" field indicates that the record concerns an organization located in the United Kingdom, the "Postal Code" field should have a specific format of alphanumeric characters.

Validity tests: In still other cases, fields can take only a limited range of values, or must have a predetermined format. By matching the actual value to the allowable values, we can detect errors. Element validity tests determine whether the values of various fields, considered individually, are acceptable. For example, on a job application, the only acceptable values for the data element "Applicant Sex" are "M" or "F." Validity tests against files (or tables) require the system to check the values in the input record against a table or file of acceptable values. For example, if a field is supposed to contain a valid U.S. postal abbreviation for a state, "AZ" would be valid but "A2" would not. A good example of this test, which is common in many systems, is the looking up of the transaction account number on the master file to verify that it exists.

4.4.3 Is data conversion properly controlled?

The segment of the decision tree extracted as Figure 4.6 is concerned with controls over the conversion of data, for example, conversion from a handwritten form to a machine-readable form. The question, of course, is, How can we determine that the output of the conversion is correct? How do we know that no data has been added, deleted, or modified, either accidentally or deliberately? The tests suggested on this tree are not meant to represent an exhaustive list but do represent the most frequently used methods. Explanations of these controls follow.

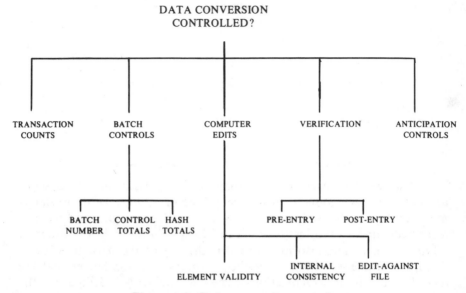

Figure 4.6. Data conversion controls.

Anticipation controls work by allowing the computer (or the I/O control function) to know in advance some characteristic of the input, and to compare the anticipated characteristic to the actually received value. There are two major applications of anticipation control: First, when input forms can be pre-numbered, the system can be programmed to assure that all forms are accounted for. Depending on the criticality of the application, it may be desirable either to report an out-of-sequence number or to suspend processing if an out-of-sequence number is encountered. Some form of "voiding" transaction may be necessary to account for spoiled forms. Note, too, that the system should be able to detect repeated numbers. The second application of anticipation controls occurs when serial batch numbering is used instead of pre-numbered forms. In this case, every department sequentially numbers each batch that it submits to DP. For example, a batch number of 21-426 indicates that the batch is the 426th submitted by department 21 this year. Should an abnormal condition be detected by the system (that is, a batch number out of sequence or repeated), appropriate action can be taken. Obviously, these controls are designed to make it more difficult to enter unauthorized transactions or batches into the system.

Like anticipation controls, the various forms of *batch controls* are all designed to reduce the probability of entering incorrect information. *Batch numbering* is a simple technique for insuring that transaction batches are not lost. Essentially, each batch is serially numbered, and the processor checks to make sure that all numbers are accounted for and in order. In a variation, various departments may each have their own serial numbering scheme. If a payroll batch is numbered PAY-483, the system would accept the batch only if the previous payroll batch received by the system were PAY-482.

Control totals help to avoid errors in data entry. Various input fields (for example, check amount or quantity received) are added on all transactions and a total arrived at. In other cases, control totals may be developed for numbers that would normally never be added (account numbers or social security numbers, for example). This latter type of control is called a *hash total.* In either case, both the expected totals and the individual transactions are passed to the system. The system recalculates totals from individual records received and compares them to expected totals. If they do not match, an error has been detected — perhaps not all the transactions were processed before.

Analysts often forget the necessity of defining the trade-offs between the added security of additional totals and the added work of calculating them for each batch submitted for processing. For example, it might seem like a good idea to require the personnel department to provide a hash total of social security numbers for each batch of transactions. But the work involved in adding a series of nine-digit numbers may not be worth it. Even if it is worthwhile in objective terms, the personnel department staff may object so vociferously that it may be wise to devise a simpler alternative (such as post-entry verification of the transactions processed by the system).

As the name implies, *transaction counts* are nothing more than keeping track of the number of transactions that *should* have been processed by a system. If the payroll department received 547 payroll updates today, the DP department should receive the same number for processing tonight (assuming none were rejected in the payroll department). If the count is off, something is probably wrong. Either a transaction has been lost, or an extra one added.

Pre-entry verification is the examination of the results of the conversion process before using the data. For example, a payroll system might generate a payroll change edit report for review prior to actually updating the payroll master file. This pre-review enables errors to be caught before they are processed and, if diligently carried out, can avoid a great deal of processing to back out errors. Alternatively, in *post-entry verification,* the system performs the processing first and then checks for data entry errors.

The three major types of so-called *computer edits* are, in a sense, double duty controls. They can detect errors regardless of whether the error was generated in the data conversion process or simply by a wrong input. Computer edits have already been explained in Section 4.4.2.

4.4.4 Is internal process movement controlled?

As data moves through a system, it is usually subjected to a series of processes, both manual and automated. Figure 4.7 reminds us that the movement of data between processing steps should be appropriately controlled. Once a batch is readied for processing, it should immediately enter a controlled environment. That is, records of its movement should be kept, and the movement itself controlled. Often, much of this can be accomplished by nothing more complex than a logbook and signature control. As shown in Figure 4.7, there are two types of control to be considered: batch receipt controls and run-to-run controls.

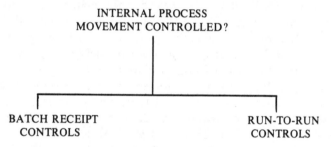

Figure 4.7. Internal process movement controls.

Batch receipt controls are used to carefully control the physical movement of transactions or files from place to place — for example, from the user's desk to the data center. Before data is moved, the person accepting it must sign a receipt. At all times, some known individual is responsible for the controlled material.

If yesterday's final accounts receivable file contained 56,834 records with a total receivable value of $17,426,882.07, then today's initially input A/R file had better have exactly the same value and count. If it doesn't, either you have mounted or read the wrong file, or you have a big problem (unauthorized changes!). Either way, if you don't check, you'll never know. This problem requires a *run-to-run control test;* there are two ways to perform this kind of test. First, you could embed the control totals within the file. Unfortunately, doing so is not the strongest control, as anyone gaining access to the file could easily modify the embedded control totals to give the appearance of normality. It is often more effective to have a separate, highly controlled "controls file" that is not as accessible as the data files.

4.4.5 Are the correction of errors and the resubmission of corrected transactions controlled?

For some reason that I have never been able to determine, systems analysts rarely give attention to error and resubmission controls. Simply put, if an input record is rejected from the system, the record must be fixed and re-entered into the proper part of the system. In some applications, this is an absolutely vital function. For example, in banking, if a deposit transaction is rejected, it is necessary to correct and resubmit it before the nightly account posting run. Otherwise, the system may bounce a number of checks for which there are sufficient funds. In other cases, there may be no legal requirement for immediate posting, but I strongly recommend that you consider the need for correction and resubmission controls for *every* input data stream. Figure 4.8 indicates the two types of error correction and resubmission controls.

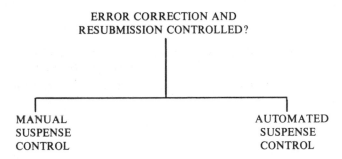

Figure 4.8. Error correction and resubmission controls.

A *manual suspense control* is a physical log, in the form of a book or of control tickets, in which each rejected transaction is listed, along with the date and/or time by which the transaction is to be corrected and re-entered. If the corrected transaction isn't received by the due date or time (or if it isn't canceled to indicate that it will not be re-entered), the operator of the manual suspense control reports the problem and follows up on the missing transaction. For example, the suspense control clerk might call the responsible party to ask why the transaction is being delayed.

In an *automated suspense control,* the same record keeping, reporting, and following up is performed, only it is done by the computer. Rejects go onto a suspense file; if they are not "cleared" from the file by re-entry or cancellation in a timely fashion, the system takes appropriate action to follow up on the problem.

4.5 Processing controls

At this point, you will have considered all of the controls for the input streams of your system. Having decided upon an appropriate level of control for the inputs, you can then consider the controls over the processing of those inputs. In Figure 4.9, the tree shows three major types of processing controls: run-to-run controls, file and operator controls, and limit and reasonableness tests. Let's look at each in turn.

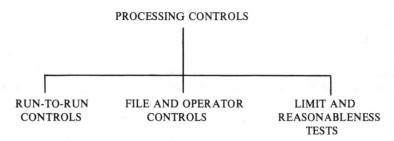

Figure 4.9. Major processing controls.

We've briefly discussed run-to-run controls before, but let me define the two aspects of these controls more formally. Run-to-run controls consist of data generation controls and verification controls (see Figure 4.10).

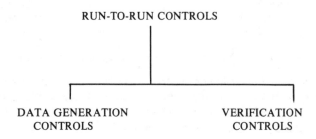

Figure 4.10. Run-to-run controls.

Data generation controls insure that you are using the correct version of the file. For example, if today is January 12 and if the system runs daily, you want to be certain that the file you're going to process was created on January 11. How you do this will differ, depending in part on your hardware and software. You may be able to use a standard vendor-provided system that keeps track of the different versions of your files. In other cases, you may have to put automated tests within your application or you may be limited to manual procedures, as described in the next section of the decision tree and as shown in Figure 4.11.

Verification controls are the control totals discussed in Section 4.4.4 that insure that the totals or record counts for the end of the prior run match the opening totals for the current run.

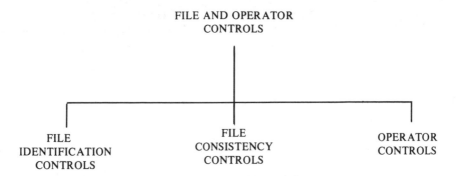

FILE AND OPERATOR
CONTROLS

FILE
IDENTIFICATION
CONTROLS

FILE
CONSISTENCY
CONTROLS

OPERATOR
CONTROLS

Figure 4.11. File and operator controls.

The controls in Figure 4.11 are actions that the operator can take to insure that the system is processing the right files and data. The control could be as simple as checking the tape or disk label, for instance. My major point is to warn of a danger inherent in operator controls: Too often, the operating system enables operators to make disastrous errors. For example, let's say that the operator received the following message on the console:

TAPE LABEL ERROR
Enter "1" to retry, "2" to abort, "3" to accept.

Under what circumstances do you want the operator to type in "3"? You probably *never* want the operator to ignore and override this message. Since the vast majority of shops don't have the resources either to disable option 3 or to subject it to additional (password) control, prevention is a matter of operator training and of reviewing the console log to reduce the probability of undetected operator-induced error.

The third and final kind of processing control, the so-called *limit and reasonableness tests,* are used during processing to insure that everything is proceeding normally. The tests listed in Figure 4.12 are self-explanatory. Let me merely point out that these are powerful quality control tools. If built into a system properly, they will work efficiently and silently to safeguard your data. You should expect to hear from these tests only when something bad happens. It's a good feeling (especially from the user's viewpoint) just to know they are there, and I firmly believe that these controls are highly cost effective. The cost to repair even one posting of an unbalanced transaction to your firm's general ledger system can be huge in comparison to the cost of the controls that can prevent such an unfortunate event from occurring in the first place.

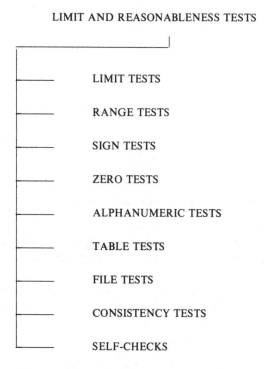

LIMIT AND REASONABLENESS TESTS

- LIMIT TESTS
- RANGE TESTS
- SIGN TESTS
- ZERO TESTS
- ALPHANUMERIC TESTS
- TABLE TESTS
- FILE TESTS
- CONSISTENCY TESTS
- SELF-CHECKS

Figure 4.12. Limit and reasonableness tests.

4.6 Output controls

Finally, there are three types of output controls to be considered, as shown in Figure 4.13.

Control totals verify the correctness of the outputs. For example, if an accounts payable system generates 236 checks with an expected total value of $395,434.99, we could physically add the checks to be certain that that is the actual value of the checks that were generated.

Verification controls coordinate physical and system processes. For example, to avoid unauthorized loss of blank checks, we commonly have the computer keep track of the expected serial numbers of preprinted checks and to print the expected number on the check. Thus, the check with preprinted number 503462 must have the same number printed on it by the computer. In other words, the same number appears on the check twice. If the numbers differ, something is wrong!

Distribution controls insure that once prepared, outputs are delivered to authorized recipients. For example, users may be required to sign for their reports. In other cases, in order to receive this week's report, a user must return last week's version. Distribution usually contains significant, but unrecognized weaknesses.

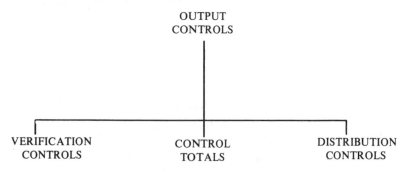

Figure 4.13. Output controls.

I remember the case of a client who had a computer center with the security of Fort Knox: cameras, badge locks, magnetometers, and so forth. The company did not hesitate to spend huge sums of money to secure the computer center. Unfortunately, management never thought about what happened to the data after it left the data center. I found a mail cart riding unattended in the elevator of a public building. The cart contained highly confidential company sales data. Because the cart had a defective wheel (it shook violently when pushed, like a broken supermarket shopping cart), the mail clerk decided that it was too much trouble to push it around and left it in the elevator, carrying by hand the deliveries for a single floor at a time, and calling for the elevator when it was time to go to the next floor. Amazing! The company had spent more than $100,000 to build a secure facility, but was undone by a seventeen-year-old kid with a busted cart.

4.7 Conclusion

This brings to a close our review of the decision tree as an analytic tool for the development of controls and of the basic controls available to the developer and maintainer of systems. In the next chapter, I introduce an approach to building controls into systems called *phase-related control,* which can be used in conjunction with the decision tree.

5 | Basic Concepts of Phase-Related Control

The reason that systems control isn't routinely considered by developers and others is that there hasn't been a conceptual framework for such consideration. There appears to be no standard set of rules to be followed in considering controls; systems developers don't even know where to begin. In the following sections, I offer you a way of breaking the big problem of building the controls into a series of smaller, simpler, and manageable problems. This "divide and conquer" philosophy for controls is embodied in the technique called *phase-related control* (PRC) and is the same philosophy that underlies structured systems development. Phase-related control is the process of identifying, specifying, and documenting the internal controls appropriate to each stage of the systems development life cycle. In this chapter, we review the basic concepts of phase-related control and provide you with a graphic road map of the technique.

5.1 Phase-related control

Phase-related control provides the basis for *overt* consideration and specification of control. That may not seem like too big a breakthrough, but I assure you that it is.

The concept of following a methodology for considering, selecting, and installing controls is important. Traditionally, we have not had such a methodology, and therefore, our systems have been poorly controlled. In the overwhelming majority of systems development projects, developers give little or no consideration to controls during the systems analysis phase of the life cycle. Even in those instances when they do, there is usually no framework available to help assure that they perform a complete job of control evaluation. Indeed, we can draw a parallel between PRC and structured analysis. A major advantage of structured

70

analysis is that it provides a way other than running out of time or money to know that you're done with analysis. Similarly, PRC offers a framework by which you can determine controls in your system throughout the systems development life cycle.

Controls relating to an application can be divided into three types: analysis-time controls, design-time controls, and implementation-time controls. Such a division makes sense because it brings control development into line with the systems development life cycle. For example, since in structured systems development we don't divide a system into production runs until we begin the packaging process at the analysis/design interface, it doesn't make sense to build run-to-run controls into a system before then.* And in structured systems development we don't concern ourselves with input/output controls until we have at least determined the automation boundary. In short, if we are concerned with controlling a structured system, we should follow the structured development principle that calls for postponing decisions concerning particular physical processes until the logical system is well understood.

In this and the next three chapters, I want to show you how to build effective controls into your company's application systems. To do that, I provide the tools and I emphasize the importance of raising your organization's *control consciousness*. Used together, phase-related control and the decision tree in Chapter 4 will provide you with a plan for developing controls in your systems.

5.2 Overview

Figure 5.1 presents an overview, in data flow diagram form, of the four tasks composing the phase-related control technique. We begin our consideration of Figure 5.1 at bubble 1, Define Analysis-Time Controls, a process that is treated in detail in Chapter 6. For now, we see that it has three inputs and three outputs. The inputs are the following:

1.   *Information on control requirements.* This input tells about the need for security and control in the system. How critical is the information that is being processed? How valuable is it? How adequate are the controls in the present system? Are more needed, or perhaps fewer?

---

*I use the term *production runs* to mean a separately executed computer program that is run as part of a series of programs, each of which receives data from the program executed before it and passes data to the program after it.

2. *Information on current operations.* How is the current system controlled? What mechanisms exist to prevent errors and omissions by workers? In short, how do you know that what the system tells you is correct?

3. *Information on new requirements.* What will the new system do that the current one doesn't? What controls will those new functions need?

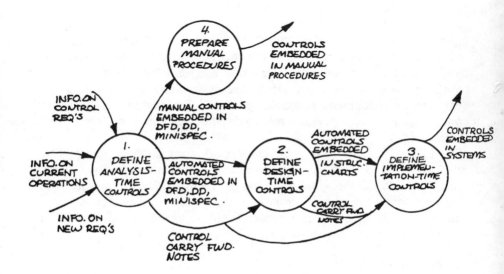

Figure 5.1. Overview of the PRC technique.

The three outputs from bubble 1 follow:

1. *Manual controls.* One of the great strengths of structured analysis is that it forces the analyst to consider systems in their entirety, including functions on both sides of the man-machine boundary. Premature setting of the man-machine boundary has traditionally resulted in a concentration of functions on the machine side of the boundary, and a playing down (often more a disregard) of functions on the human side. With structured analysis, however, we can more easily meet our objective of building controls appropriate to the total system, rather than just the automated portion. When the system is broken into human- and

machine-operated segments, the human control components are sent to whoever is writing the manual procedures.

The manual controls over the system will be embedded in the DFDs and data dictionary, among other tools. In short, if the controls are to be built into the system, they must appear as an integral part of the documentation of the system. Just how that is done will be clear by the time you've completed Chapter 6.

2. *Automated controls.* These are the controls on the computer side of the man-machine boundary. Just as with the controls on the human side, they are given in the structured specification, using the tools of structured analysis. As part of the target specification, they are passed forward to the structured design process.

3. *Control carry-forward notes.* The control carry-forward notes are a way for analysts to tell designers and implementors about control-related issues that they should consider in doing their work. The notes enable the analyst to communicate to the designer a design-time control identified during analysis. Since we clearly can't build the information into the DFDs (if we could, we would be dealing with an analysis-time control), we need some form of documentation to pass control-related information forward from analysis to design — or even to implementation. These notes are just such a tool.

In bubble 2, Define Design-Time Controls, we create a control structure to support the module hierarchy that will represent the automated system. We will be considering this process in Chapter 7. But as an overview, these are the inputs of bubble 2:

1. *Controls contained in the analysis specifications.* These are the analysis-time controls that have been passed forward to the design phase, in the form of DFD, data dictionary, and minispecification entries.

2. *Control carry-forward notes.* These are the notes from the analysis team to the design team concerning controls to be specified during the design.

The outputs of bubble 2 are the following:

1. *Controls embedded in the structure charts and module specifications.* The primary output of the design-time control process is the set of controls built into the design documentation. These controls represent both the analysis-time controls further detailed during the design, and the design-time controls defined during the design phase.

2. *Control carry-forward notes.* These are the notes on control issues to be communicated to the implementation team. They join any notes for the implementation team prepared by the analysts.

Bubble 3, Define Implementation-Time Controls, is the point at which the previously identified controls are built along with any controls newly specified during the implementation phase. This process has two inputs, which we have seen before: the controls embedded in the design specification, and the control carry-forward notes prepared in the analysis and design phases of the systems development process. The output, of course, is the resultant well-controlled system.

Meanwhile, bubble 4, Prepare Manual Procedures, is the place where the controls embedded on the data flow diagrams, data dictionary, and minispecifications of the manually operated portions of the new system are processed. Like the rest of the manual part of the system, the controls must be converted into specific instructions for those who will be responsible for carrying them out. As in the automated part of the system, the controls become an essential, integrated part of the system.

The next three chapters show you how phase-related control works, and how you can integrate the PRC technique into your systems development life cycle, thereby insuring that controls are adequately considered. But before doing so, honesty requires me to give you several warnings.

5.3 Warning: control zone ahead

Having helped organizations raise their control consciousness, I know you should expect some resistance to an increased emphasis on internal control in your organization's systems, along with other problems. Specifically, there are four problems that seem to occur almost everywhere. Be aware of them so that you can develop a plan to handle them if they occur in your shop.

5.3.1 Warning: It's going to cost you

Controls carry a price. In addition to the obvious cost of the effort required for their development, costs associated with system complexity, inefficiency, and constraints will stimulate complaints.

First is the complaint that *controls make the system more complex.* True, incorporating controls probably requires more analysis, more design, and more code, but doing so results in a system that does more things. I'm all for recommending that you plan to install the minimum set of controls necessary for them to be effective, but what's the value of a simple system *without* control? This complexity argument arises because when it becomes necessary to retrofit controls into existing systems, complexity *can* be a problem. But when controls are designed into a system from the start, the amount of complexity will be less, and it will be more than made up for by increased accuracy and reliability.

Next comes the complaint that *controls make the system inefficient.* Obviously, the execution of control-related code and the performance of manual controls take time. I suppose that in purely statistical terms those tasks reduce efficiency, but I believe that any competent manager or DP professional would reject this argument as specious. The reason is that efficiency is almost *never* the most basic consideration in systems design — effectiveness is. Once you've met that objective, you may want to consider efficiency. But recognize that at today's computer speeds it isn't always cost effective to spend a lot of people time to save a little computer time.

A third complaint is that *controls constrain the system.* Of course they constrain the system. Every systems requirement does. So what? All that controls do is to force you not to lose control of assets. That sounds to me like good business, *not* like an unreasonable constraint.

5.3.2 Warning: Beware of ostriches

During systems development, many DP people intensely dislike thinking about anything associated with auditing. I think this dislike stems from the bad experiences suffered during past audits. The old-timers in the shop have gone through a lot of aggravating audits, and newcomers hear about the misery of audits through the grapevine. In any case, the bad feelings cause systems developers to want to forget about the inevitability of future audits.

This sounds a lot like the psychological ego defense mechanism known as *repression,* and it can cause developers to take the exact actions guaranteed to result in bad auditing reports. It leads to formation of a vicious cycle, as shown in Figure 5.2.

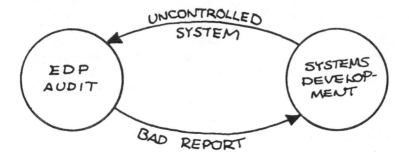

Figure 5.2. Vicious cycle of development and auditing.

The cycle is composed of these events:

- An EDP audit results in a bad report, which leads to much aggravation for systems developers as they answer the charges and findings made in their reports.

- Systems developers discover that in the long run management doesn't impose any negative consequences for poor controls or for poor auditing reports. So they don't have to dredge up those unpleasant memories — and unpleasant emotions — relating to audits.

- Knowing that they can safely ignore controls, the DP staff members develop even more poorly controlled systems.

- And that results in another negative auditing report, which causes more negative emotions, which strengthens the desire to avoid thinking about audits, which leads to more poorly controlled systems.

Traditional systems development life cycle techniques haven't done anything to break us of our bad habits; we have been able to get away with poor controls for too long.

5.3.3 Warning: Users can be indifferent to controls

Frequently, users have to be reminded of the need for control. They may assume that the DP people are taking care of the controls, so they can ignore them. Or, they may not recognize the need for controls in their new system. If necessary, the DP project leader should point out to the user that if the system mismanages the assets, everyone suffers.

Once while I was working on the development of a multi-bank electronic funds transfer project, a representative from one of the banks expressed the belief that there was no need to issue secret codes to customers with cash machine cards. "Why complicate things?" he asked. "Our customers shouldn't be forced to remember some crazy number." When asked how we could positively identify the cash machine user as the authorized customer, he answered, "Simple. Only the customer will have the activator card." Great. When someone suggested that if he had his way he might be named Man of the Year by the mugger's union, it went right over his head.

5.3.4 *Warning: It isn't a game!*

Sometimes, auditors and quality assurance people have to be reminded that problem avoidance beats problem resolution every time. Auditors and quality assurance people have their share of practitioners who believe that to be successful, they have to find lots of problems. There are those who would rather come in at the end of systems development and publish a scathing report than provide counsel *during* the development process and so avoid the problems. All I can say is these people should be recognized as unprofessional, and action should be taken to either reform or remove them.

5.4 Summary

In this chapter, I've introduced you to the basic concept of phase-related control — namely, the division of the problem of control into constituent parts. In the next chapter, we begin a phase-by-phase review of the major stages in the systems development process to see how we can apply the principles of phase-related control, how we can best identify where controls are needed, and how we can determine which controls are appropriate under various circumstances.

6 | Modeling Controls During the Analysis Phase

In Chapter 4, I presented a general model of application controls, based on the decision tree. By using the tree, you can identify all types of controls, many of which are analysis-time controls. In this chapter, we concentrate on analysis-time controls and on how you can build controls into your systems during the structured analysis process.

What controls should be specified during analysis? The answer is that we should specify those controls that represent business policy, and that exist independently of the particular way the system is to be implemented. (These are the controls that would be necessary whether the system were manual or automated, for example, or on-line or batch.) In other words, analysis-time controls (ATCs) include those *logical* policies that ensure the accuracy, completeness, and security of processing; they are modeled using the tools and concepts of structured analysis.

Although the primary analysis-time controls carry out logical policies, some analysis-time controls are implementation dependent. These controls are specified at the end of the analysis phase to meet stated physical constraints. For example, consider the following user requirement:

User Requirement: The internal audit department is to receive a report detailing all accepted file maintenance update transactions posted to the payroll master file.

Figure 6.1 shows one way to model this requirement. This figure illustrates the kind of control that you *must* consider during analysis, because of these three reasons: It represents a user policy; it specifies what is to be done, not how it is to be done (it could, after all, be a manual process); and it is no different conceptually from any other user policy that we consider as a part of structured analysis.

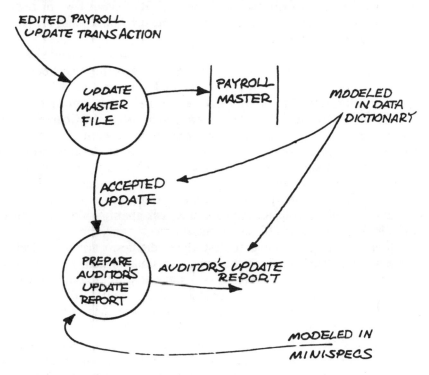

Figure 6.1. Model of an audit trail report.

6.1 Sources of analysis-time controls

Systems analysts can use four different sources to identify controls that belong in the new system: stated user policy, unstated user policy, the current system, and external constraints. I briefly describe each below.

The first source the analyst should turn to is *stated user policy.* I know that in the eyes of some systems analysts, the following statement is somewhat blasphemous: The best way to begin to determine the controls needed in a system is to ask the users about the need for controls. Users have a genuine stake in the new system as well as thorough knowledge of their own requirements. Now, they may not *think* that they know a lot about controls, because they probably don't think of their activities in terms of controls. But if you ask the right questions, they can give you a picture of the way the system should operate in order for them to feel secure. For example, ask them how they handle errors in the present system. Ask them about the kinds of errors or problems that they suspect they don't know about (that is, those that are slipping through undetected). Ask about laws or regulations that affect the way system processes must be done, and ask about the value and criticality of the data.

I'm not telling you to expect a masterful, fully integrated set of control requirements from users; I'm merely suggesting that liberal use of the question, But how do you know that it's correct?, will bring a wealth of information if asked of the right users at the right times.

Second, you must discover *unstated user policy.* In Chapter 1, we saw that users expect comprehensive controls to be built into their systems without their ever mentioning controls in discussions with the analysis team. Users expect that controls will be built into the system automatically simply because it is good business to do so. Because users believe this, they probably won't mention all of the control requirements even if you question them or ask them to do so. You've got to look for the unstated requirements.

For example, the need to test check digits on account numbers may never be stated, because the present manual system may not have facilities to permit it. But users may assume that an automated system tests check digits as a matter of course and that you don't need to be told to build such tests into the system. And you may not do so, but the users won't know that you didn't. Since they may well assume that such controls are a part of the computer itself, it won't occur to them to test the controls. So, a system with weak controls can go into operation with the user firmly believing that the controls are good. You can't allow such assumptions to be made. You must learn the system — and understand the problem — well enough to challenge the unstated assumptions of the users and turn unstated requirements into stated ones.

Third, you must study and understand *the current system.* New systems tend to do many of the same things as the systems they replace. Of course, they may do them differently (via a terminal, for example, rather than through batch-produced reports). So, while the specific controls in the new system may differ from those in the old system, there are going to be overlaps, particularly with regard to analysis-time controls (most of which are independent of implementation and architecture). Many, if not most, of the analysis-time controls needed for the new system are present in the old system. But you have to look for them, and you have to recognize them as controls and to assess their suitability for transplantation into the new system.

Finally, never forget the potential impact of *external constraints*. Various laws and regulations can directly affect a system — not just government regulations, but such rules that exist, for example, between corporations in a conglomerate, or banks participating in an automated clearinghouse. If your system is required to produce certain information or reports, there should be controls to assure that the restrictions are honored.

6.2 Modeling rejects

Before discussing the process of specifying controls during analysis, I want to consider a problem you may have modeling controls according to the structured analysis method. Consider this example:

User Requirement: Report all rejected payroll transactions on the Payroll Exception Report.

Here's the problem: How can we model this requirement (if, indeed, we should model it) without violating the structured analysis guideline of not showing detailed processing of trivial rejects on DFDs? (A *trivial* reject does not require undoing of previous work in the course of processing the rejection.) If we didn't have the requirement for reporting the rejected transactions, we could model the payroll edit as shown in Figure 6.2.

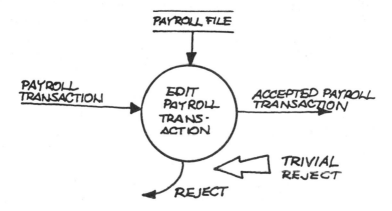

Figure 6.2. Incorrect consideration of reject as being trivial.

Now, if we consider the production of the exception report to be part of the editing process, rather than part of reject processing, the solution is simple, as shown in Figure 6.3. Of course, we have to model the exception report in the data dictionary, and model its production in the minispecs that describe the editing bubble (or, more likely, the lower-level children of this bubble).

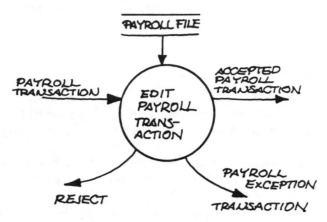

Figure 6.3. Acceptable model of an exception report.

Modeling the report works because the control that we are modeling (production of a report documenting rejected transactions) is *independent* of the rejects themselves. The creation of the report is a part of the processing that results from certain incoming transactions being turned into rejects. Therefore, it can be modeled without violating the principles of structured analysis.

Now consider the following user policy, which presents a more complex problem for control.

Error Correction Policy: If a transaction is rejected because there is no matching employee number, review it. Call the originator to determine if the name is correct. If it is, refer to the employee list to determine the correct employee number, and resubmit it.

The question is whether it is valid to model this; the answer depends upon your point of view. From the point of view of the processor of the edit process (for example, the computer), we are dealing with a trivial reject, as shown in Figure 6.4. Of course, we aren't modeling from the point of view of the processor, as most systems analysts do. We are modeling the entire process, both its automated and manual parts — in this case, the entire payroll process, as in Figure 6.5.

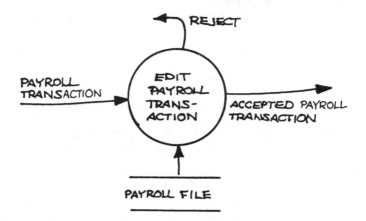

Figure 6.4. Payroll edit reject from viewpoint of automated system.

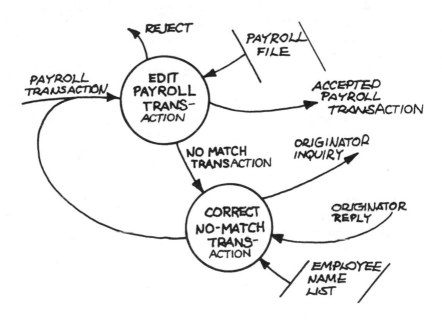

Figure 6.5. Correct view of the total system.

Until we examine the transaction in the Correct No-Match Transactions bubble and determine that we can't fix it, it isn't a reject.
When we speak of rejects, we really mean *net* rejects, rejects that leave
the system entirely. True, the original edit is likely to be done by a
computer, while the correction will be accomplished by a clerk, but this
is irrelevant right now. During analysis, we try not to set the automation details (sometimes called the man-machine boundary). Therefore,
we can't dismiss rejected transactions as trivial rejects simply because
they are processed manually.

6.3 Considering controls in the structured analysis process

A major weakness of traditional analysis methods is the emphasis
on automated portions of the system to the detriment of manual controls. By contrast, structured analysis forces the analyst to give equal
consideration to processes on both sides of the man-machine boundary
by not declaring this boundary until the end of the analysis phase.
Internal control and security in a system can be considered and evaluated only in light of "weak-link theory." Weak-link theory reminds us
that regardless of how much time, money, effort, and sophistication are
reflected in the controls over automated portions of a system, if the
controls over manual processes are weak, the controls over the total
system are weak. In my experience, many systems have an elaborate
facade of automated controls built into them, a fact that does not make
them well-controlled systems.

For example, if we develop a control calling for a payroll system
to print a control number on each check, the same number as the preprinted check number (to prevent unauthorized removal of checks),
the automated control is useless unless we develop a manual control to
determine that the preprinted and control numbers are the same. In
fact, without the manual control, the automated control is likely to be
worse than useless, because the very existence of an automated control
may provide unwarranted confidence in the accuracy or completeness of
processing.

The systems development team has five functions to perform in
assuring control during the process of structured analysis:

- to identify, understand, and model the controls in the
  current (old physical) system

- to understand and model the controls in the old logical
  system

- to identify and understand the control implications of new or modified systems requirements

- to model the controls necessary for the new system (as represented by the new physical system model)

- to prepare carry-forward control constraints for subsequent phases of the systems development process

Taken together, these functions provide a way to model controls during analysis. In the next five sections, each of these functions is discussed.

6.3.1 Modeling controls in the current system

How do you identify controls in the old physical system? You use the decision tree tool given in Chapter 4. By following the branches of the tree, you evaluate one at a time each net input, each net output, and each major processing stream shown on the current physical model of the system. Carrying out this process will enable you to recognize the controls already in the current system and will indicate any controls that should be there but are not. Don't just accept the controls already in the system; they may not be effective. The decision tree will help you decide which current controls are not appropriate and which are.

I must point out that the decision tree identifies *all of the major controls in the system, not just the analysis-time controls.* So at some point, as discussed in Section 6.3.5, the analysis-time controls must be separated from the design-time and implementation-time controls.

As soon as you find a control — either one in the current system or one that should be there — model it. Controls should be modeled with the same degree of detail as the rest of the current physical system. Model the controls in the same way you would model any other process that you are analyzing. For example, Figure 6.6 shows use of a data flow diagram to model the process by which we verify that file maintenance transactions are authorized. Note in this example I assumed that a transaction that did not pass the verification tests could be treated as a trivial reject. When you prepare your analysis models, don't blindly make such assumptions. You must determine whether there are resubmission controls that should be built into the model.

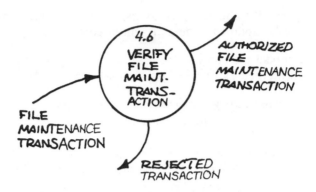

Figure 6.6. Pre-processing authorization test.

A minispecification, such as the one below, should accompany the DFD to tell how the verification process works.

MINISPEC 4.6 – PRE-PROCESSING AUTHORIZATION TEST

> Use Authorization-Code and Department
> > to look up Security-Code in security table
>
> IF Security-Code from table equals Security-Code
> > from the file maintenance transaction
>
> THEN issue Authorized-File-Maintenance-Transaction
>
> ELSE issue Rejected-Transaction

Similarly, we could model batch balancing controls, as shown in Figure 6.7. (The same warning concerning trivial rejects applies.)

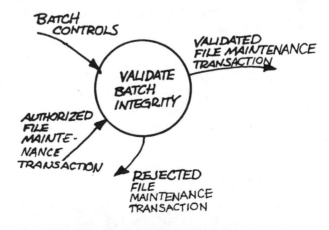

Figure 6.7. Batch control test.

6.3.2 Logical modeling

There comes a time in every structured analysis project when the process known as *logical modeling* or *logicalization* occurs. In this process, we separate the *true requirements* of a system — those things that a system must do regardless of the particular way in which the system is built — from those actions that depend on how the system is built. By using logical modeling, we avoid detailed questions on implementation by relegating them to a later stage in the development process. Logical modeling prevents projects from getting bogged down because project members concentrate on details before all the general parameters are set. If project members are too busy with the details, the new system will never get built.

An example of a logical requirement of a system is an airline reservation system's need to respond to seat availability requests whether the system is implemented as a massive on-line, real-time application, a distributed minicomputer network, or a manual system of reservations posted on huge blackboards. On the other hand, batch controls are not logical, since a system only has them because the particular implementation chosen requires that the data be batched for periodic input. At least conceptually, the same system could have been designed to accept input on-line and continuously.

In other words, among all of the controls observed in a system, some controls have logical equivalents while others don't. Those that do are the analysis-time controls that will remain in the old logical model. They are concerned with basic business policy, such as exception reports and edits. For example, the statement "Do not accept a check from a customer who has had two checks returned in the past year" clearly is a control that is equally applicable whether the system being modeled is fully manual or fully automated. Other controls don't have a logical equivalent. For example, any control that is solely concerned with the transportation or conversion of data, or that covers the controls over man-machine interface points and run-to-run control points won't appear in the logical model. If in the previous stage you decided such a control was appropriate to the system, your models and notes for that control are placed in the carry-forward notes for consideration in a later stage. Improper controls are discarded.

6.3.3 Adding new requirements to the model

The transition from the current logical model to the new logical model consists of manipulating the current logical model by adding, deleting, or modifying functions to achieve the user's objectives. Since they are a part of the logical model, these changes represent business policy, and some of them may well have significant control consequences.

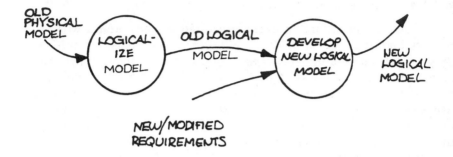

Figure 6.8. Modifying the logical model.

Consider an example: Your little shop that offers sales and service on portable Whiz-Bangs is becoming so successful that you want to accept payment by credit cards. What logical controls do you need?

While I don't intend to offer a complete list, I do suggest you start with the following controls: First, check cards to be sure they haven't expired. Second, if a purchase is over a predetermined limit, verify the transaction with the credit card company. Third, refuse a cash refund if the charged merchandise is returned. Fourth, check the signature on the sales slip against that on the card. Finally, assure that transaction records for all credit card purchases are transmitted to the card-issuing company for credit to your account.

Note that in each case, the policy tells *what* to do, not *how* to do it. Nowhere did I indicate that the verification with the card issuer would be manual or automated. Right now, during analysis, it doesn't matter.

Clearly, here is another point in the development process when the decision tree described in Chapter 4 comes in handy. You can examine the new logical policy to determine what control measures would be appropriate. For example, if a new input is involved, the decision tree will tell you to decide whether the input needs authorization. If it does, you can select the appropriate type of test from those suggested by the tree.

6.3.4 Let's get physical

After building the new logical model, we've finally reached the point of specifying the controls for the new physical system. This involves putting constraints into the logical model that you've created. With regard to controls, this constraining or *physicalization* process has three tasks:

- giving physical reality to the logical controls

- adding physical controls necessary to support physical processes

- adding the controls required by particular constraints

Giving physical reality to logical controls means making the changes needed to make a control operate in the real world. To accomplish this and to add the other analysis-time physical controls, you must first set the man-machine boundary. The method for determining the boundary is well described in the literature of structured analysis,* but for our purposes, remember the following: As processes and dataflows are added to the model to provide necessary communication and data translation across the man-machine boundary, each must be examined to determine the types of controls needed to support it. This is the process of identifying input streams, significant processing, and output streams, and evaluating them with the decision tree, as explained in Chapter 4.

Using the decision tree, ask how effectively each stream of data and purely physical process is controlled. Based on the value, sensitivity, and criticality of the assets involved, more or less control may be needed. You should add the bubbles, dataflows, and data stores required to achieve the appropriate degree of control. For example, you may determine that a particular input in the actual physical system will be batched for nightly entry. This would lead you to consider the controls necessary to assure that each batch is complete and correct, and that all batches are received.

Your sources for information on those controls appropriate to the physicalized systems should include these five:

- *Controls in the present system:* As stated before, the new physical system resembles the old physical system in many respects, and you may well find that some of the internal controls remain perfectly adequate. If so, why not leave them in place? Or, possibly, certain present system controls can be modified to meet your requirements. In both cases, retaining aspects of the current system helps to reduce the retraining burden on users, and may make the new system less threatening to them.

---

*See T. DeMarco, *Structured Analysis and System Specification* (New York: Yourdon Press, 1978), pp. 265-71; and B. Dickinson, *Developing Structured Systems: A Methodology Using Structured Techniques* (New York: Yourdon Press, 1981), pp. 207, 248.

- *User requirements:* Users should have a say in the system's internal control requirements, which are often set by business policy, particularly in the financial industries. For example, in the American brokerage industry, the standard way of controlling stock certificates is to capture the certificate and CUSIP numbers.*

- *Auditing and quality assurance requirements:* As a system is transformed from logical to physical, auditors may set requirements that you can model into the system. For example, they may desire that in the final system a carbon copy of each payroll change form be forwarded directly to the audit department, and that following the posting of changes to the payroll master file, a report of changes be sent to them to permit verification of the changes made.

- *Professional judgment:* Of course, the systems development professional is expected to apply his good judgment, or what we call "control consciousness."

- *Controls required by constraints:* Some constraints may imply the need for specific controls. For example, if the hardware selected has storage that can only accommodate 2,500 customer accounts, some control (manual or automated) will be needed to generate sufficient warning so that additional storage can be ordered and installed before the 2,501st customer has to be entered. For every constraint set by hardware, systems software, or management dictum, determine the control needed to assure that the constraint is respected.

6.3.5 The last step in analysis

Our final task in analysis is to consider the controls found in the present system that aren't analysis-time controls. We need a way to document these controls to carry the information forward to the next phases of the systems development process, as noted in Chapter 5. To do this, we've borrowed a term from the accounting industry. Accountants transmit information from one year's audit of a company to the next by means of documents called carry-forward working papers. As explained in Chapter 5, the term *carry-forward notes* is used to designate

---

*CUSIP is a standard industry numbering system to identify particular stock and bond issues.

the information passed from phase to phase documenting the controls observed earlier that should be taken into account by the designers and implementors. Figure 6.9 shows the movement of controls through the development process:

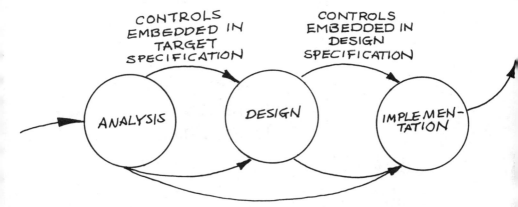

Figure 6.9. Carrying controls forward from analysis.

The carry-forward notes can take any form from formal reports to informal jottings. They are the analyst's comments to the designers and implementors on controls observed in the current system that the designer or implementor should know, design-time or implementation-time controls requested by users or auditors, and controls related to constraints that will take effect in the later phases of the project.

At the end of the structured analysis process, we have controls expressed in two ways: ATCs in the data flow diagrams, data diction-ary, and minispecs of the structured specification; and other controls in the carry-forward notes. Many of those notes are useful during design. In the next chapter, we'll look at the process of providing design-time control.

7 | Modeling Controls During the Design Phase

Design-time controls depend upon a particular systems design and result from dividing the system into physical runs (that is, independently executable jobs). In this chapter, I suggest that the decision to break an overall system into discrete runs is a design decision. However, many systems developers argue that I'm wrong, and that the division into runs is actually the last stage in systems analysis.

Guess what? It doesn't matter, because when you create runs is solely a matter of semantics. Whether you prefer to think of the run setting process as analysis or design, the steps and their general sequence are the same. For convenience, and because I believe the process to be a design activity, I characterize run-to-run controls as *design-time controls*. As I said, what you call the controls doesn't matter. That you consider them at all does matter.

7.1 Run-to-run controls

Suppose that during analysis your DP department received a memo like the one in Figure 7.1. You would probably want to begin modeling the run-to-run controls immediately. After all, you would know the system needed them even without having gotten the memo. Unfortunately, the users haven't given you much information. How do you go about modeling the run-to-run controls?

MEMO

TO: J. Smith, VP, EDP
FROM: R. Jones, VP, User Department

The auditors who were here today mentioned that they want you to put run-to-run control totals into the new system. DO IT. They'll be checking up on you.

Figure 7.1. User-stated requirement for run-to-run controls.

One way to complete the task is as follows:

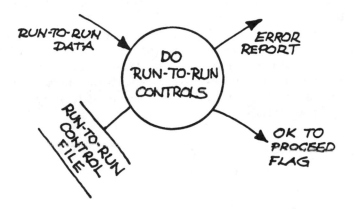

Figure 7.2. Incorrect model of run-to-run controls.

Unfortunately, Figure 7.2 is not a valid model to use during the analysis phase of systems development for three reasons:

1. We have not yet created runs.

2. The run-to-run control relates to a particular implementation (that is, a particular physical, rather than logical) policy.

3. Run-to-run controls often result in a go/no-go control flag, which we generally don't want to show in our analysis work.

Do these reasons mean that we can ignore controls that relate to particular implementations? Of course not. Run-to-run controls may represent a stated company policy and may well be operating in the present system. We should be able to model any present system and any user policy. Even if such controls aren't in the current system, if they are to be in the new system, they must be modeled. They can't just appear out of nowhere, without documentation. So, to prepare accurate models of both our present systems and our new systems, we must be able to model such controls.

The main problem with the straightforward approach used in Figure 7.2 is that we don't identify physical computer runs until the end of analysis or the beginning of design. Then we package the system by setting three physical boundaries: hardware, real-time versus on-line versus batch, and cycle (periodicity) boundaries. If we set the runs before the end of analysis, we will be making unnecessary, premature decisions about the physical implementation of the system. But how, then, can we handle controls that do depend on a particular implementation (as run-to-run controls do)?

We can handle these at the time of packaging (that is, at the beginning of design) after we have divided the system into runs. Later in the chapter, we'll have more to say about this, but Figure 7.3 illustrates how we handle such controls. We pass both the transactions and the control totals (both probably in the form of data stores) across the boundary between runs.

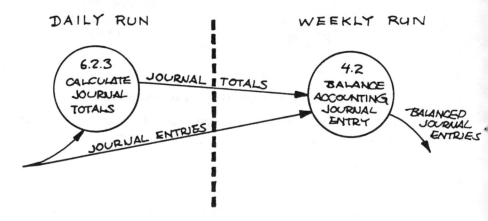

Figure 7.3. Example of run-to-run controls.

7.2 Dividing systems into runs

Some things seem to exist independently of time: children's fairy tales or adventure stories, for example. Or data flow diagrams. Data flow diagrams don't acknowledge time. They are *steady state* models, in which each bubble knows when to activate itself: Initiation and termination routines are not shown. Take a look at the DFD fragment in Figure 7.4.

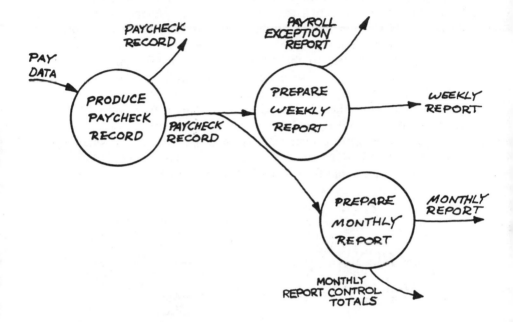

Figure 7.4. Time-independent model.

Assuming that the company produces a daily payroll, how can this diagram be correct? It is correct because by definition a DFD doesn't acknowledge timing. When the system is actually built, are you likely to have the three functions — Produce Paycheck Record, Prepare Weekly Report, and Prepare Monthly Report — in the same processing run? You probably would not, because presence of the three functions in one run would mean you would be loading code daily that you know will be used only once a month.

It is far more likely that you will divide the system into runs, each of which contains the program needed either daily, weekly, or monthly. Of course, you don't have to do this division. Not too very long ago, huge load modules (350 kilobytes and up) were the rage, and what convenience they promised! You could just run the module and it did everything, even if somewhat inefficiently. But as minicomputers and distributed processors have become increasingly popular, systems developers have seen the wisdom of limiting their load modules to those likely to be needed at a particular time.

The classic case of building everything into one module was one organization's complex budgeting system for a network of retail stores. The company kept month-by-month data for both the present and prior years' budgeted and actual revenues and costs. Every January 1, the corporate data center had to produce an extensive series of reports. It also had to archive a year's data, so that the data for the year just entered could be moved to the "Prior Year" positions in each record. This extensive set of report generators and utilities was loaded every day of the year, although it was executed only once. When asked why they did this, the analysts said that they wanted to have a "fully integrated system." What a colossal waste of resources!

Fortunately, most organizations have figured out that smaller load modules not only save time, but also ease maintenance. Figure 7.5 shows the obvious split for our DFD fragment of Figure 7.4.

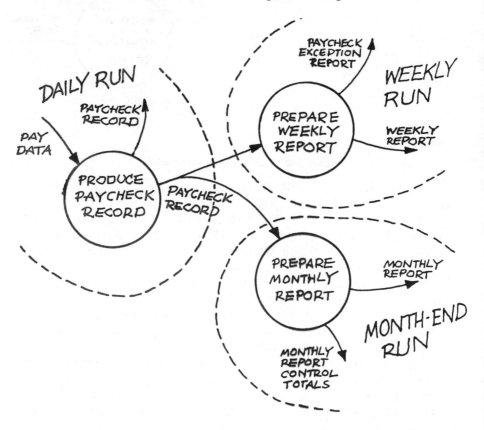

Figure 7.5. Time-dependent model.

7.3 Controlling data between runs

Now that you've divided the system into three runs, each of which is a subset of the original, there's a problem: How do you insure that all of the information from the daily runs makes its way to the weekly and monthly runs, and how do you know, when running the reports, that you have the correct inputs? Whenever data is missing or incorrect, users can be expected to find the mistake in the most inconvenient and embarrassing way (this is one of the Laws of Data Processing). The only way to avoid relying on chance compliance is to use controls — in this case, *run-to-run controls.*

As explained in Section 4.4.4, a run-to-run control operates by comparing two sums. At the end of each daily run, the system adds selected values taken from each transaction or record, thereby generating control totals. At the beginning of the weekly run, the system calculates the control totals from the daily files. The control totals from the two runs are compared; if they don't match, a file has been altered and now contains an error.

Run-to-run controls are often overlooked or given insufficient attention in development projects. There's no excuse for this since the places they are required are obvious: They're needed wherever a dataflow crosses the boundary lines between runs drawn on the DFD, as the Paycheck Record dataflow crosses the boundary between runs in Figure 7.5.

Now, consider the definition of a dataflow: It is a *pipeline through which data of known composition flows.* The transmission time — the time needed to move data through a dataflow from one process (bubble) to the next — is considered in analysis to be zero. But in the real world, of course, there is no instantaneous transmission of data from one run to another. Rather, we generally use a data store — a file — to hold the data between the runs. One run produces a file, which is passed as input to the next run, like this:

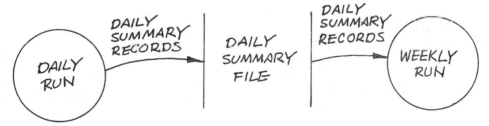

Figure 7.6. Use of a data store to cross a run-to-run boundary.

Since multi-run systems are in fact built, systems developers obviously know how to build the files that connect the runs, but they forget the control consequences of partitioning a system. Here's the rule of thumb:

> *Rule:*   When dividing a system into runs, determine control requirements for every dataflow that crosses a run-to-run boundary.

How do we build appropriate controls where data crosses run-to-run boundaries? To answer that, let's look at design-time controls.

7.4 Sources of design-time controls

By definition, design-time controls are those internal controls associated with a particular information systems design (architecture). They are generally derived from four major sources: the current system, user requirements, design judgment, and carry-forward constraints. These are similar to three of the five sources for physical analysis-time controls and are briefly discussed below.

Of course, there's no law that forces the designer of an information system to change architectures when re-designing a system. Not every batch system needs to be converted to on-line processing, and distributed processing isn't *always* the answer, regardless of the question. But you'd never believe it to look at some designers' work. There is often a drive to upgrade the technology of a system independently of any objective requirement to do so. When parts of the new system design resemble the current system design, *the current system* can be a good source of knowledge of design controls. Of course, the controls that you see in many systems are ineffective and often inefficient. They may have been built into the system after implementation, to meet auditing or quality assurance criticisms or user needs. We can avoid repeating those mistakes by building good control structures into our systems at the beginning.

A second source of information is *user requirements*. Users — and I specifically include the I/O control people as users — are the best source of information. They are the ones who have to use the systems, and they know what they need. The users may know of necessary run-to-run controls whose existence the specification doesn't indicate. For example, the users are the only ones who can tell you when single-run systems have run-to-run requirements between the two runs of the system. This can be the case if the value of yesterday's ending accounts payable file must be the same as the value of the file input today. Users also know where one file in one run should balance another file in another run. I urge you to collect such information diligently from users.

The third source of design-time controls, *design judgment,* is one of the characteristics of design specialists that induces employers to pay them high salaries. It is not unreasonable to expect a competent designer to build sufficient controls into a system. The system should be able to monitor its inputs and outputs, to detect any problems encountered, and to report them to the operators and users. No one should have to guess that a system is operating properly; users and operators should be able to rely on controls. For example, were the control totals for yesterday's ending master file the same as the totals for today's starting master file? The system should know.

Carry-forward constraints are the fourth means of obtaining information about design-time controls. These are the suggestions, observations, and notes carried forward to the design phase from the analysis phase. (See Chapter 5.)

Before reading how to model run-to-run controls, test your knowledge by taking the following mini-quiz. Question: You are in the design phase, thinking about design-time controls, but where are the analysis-time controls during the design phase? (Take a couple of minutes to think about them.) Answer: During the design phase, the analysis-time controls are built into the target specifications; they are treated like any other requirement included in the DFDs, the data dictionary, and the minispecs. They don't stand out because they're an integral part of the system.

Now let's consider how to model run-to-run controls, and some problems in doing so efficiently.

7.5 How to model run-to-run controls

Designers model run-to-run controls by adding edit features to the new physical diagram. Figure 7.7 shows a portion of such a DFD with a run-to-run control added. On a real-world DFD, the bubbles Daily Run and Weekly Run would be groups of several bubbles representing the processes handled by each run, and a dotted line would be drawn to surround each group.

Figure 7.7 provides a very general picture of a run-to-run control, but despite its general nature, it has great value. The first run (the daily run in this case) produces two data stores, one containing the actual data, the other containing the control totals relating to the data. Note that this model shows a specific Payroll Control File. This is an accurate model of what you'll find in many systems. Other systems contain a common, central control file set up so that control totals from throughout the system are stored in a single file. In a sizable number of other cases, control totals are stored within the data file, often as a special trailer record. The physical way that this is done — through a separate control file, a common control file, or an embedded control total record — isn't important. What is important is that the totals are generated and stored in a known location.

The other key part of the model is the bubble called Check Control Totals. In Figure 7.7, this bubble produces two outputs: an Exception Report and Payroll Transaction Records. These represent an arbitrary selection of outputs. For example, I could have chosen to have the system reject payroll batches or to report on all control totals. Which is correct? It all depends on the policy relating to the system. In order to model the control, the designer needs to answer these questions, When are inputs rejected? Should rejects be put into a file and controlled to assure that they are eventually returned to processing?

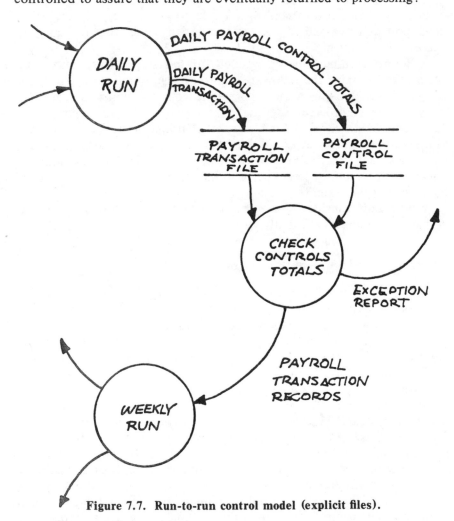

Figure 7.7. Run-to-run control model (explicit files).

The answers will vary depending on user requirements. The designer must inquire of the user to determine the policy relating to the handling of control total problems. The designer must consider that for every run-to-run total he has to account for there is the possibility that the control totals won't balance when tested. He has to know exactly what to do under such circumstances.

7.6 Control cloning

Why would anyone want to clone a control, and what does it mean? When a logical system is divided into physical runs, each split-off run may need a variety of controls, some of which will be unique, others of which will be common to several runs. The designer must be ready to deal with the case of multiple, independent runs needing identical controls. A poor policy would be to develop independent controls for each run, since that would create a problem of coordination when maintenance on a control was necessary. Imagine what would happen if the DP staff members failed to maintain one of the multiple controls. Depending on circumstances, the system could go out of control without its being known, or it could fail to operate even if everything were correct. To avoid this, we recommend that controls be cloned.

To clone a control, you create a single module or set of modules that you can make available to all runs requiring them. Maintaining a single module assures that all affected runs will have access to the latest version of all common modules.

7.7 Control considerations for structure charts

Fortunately, the same criteria that are recommended in the books on structured design to assure good design will also provide assurance that both analysis-time and design-time controls built into the DFDs and minispecs will be put into effect in the design. Interestingly, the various criteria for the goodness of structure charts (coupling, cohesion, minimization of control couples, and so forth) are all desirable for structure charts showing controls.

So, once you get into the detailed work of structured design, my advice is simply to make an effort to design the best system possible. If the controls were specified properly going into the design process, they should be properly built into the design documents, ready for implementation.

7.8 Conclusion

In the end, all designs are compromises. We trade off module size for module simplicity, and simplicity for control. There are no magic solutions to the problems associated with those trade-offs. Guidelines are all we can offer.

When you design a system — or when you review a design — keep in mind that there is a level of control that represents the absolute minimum needed to safeguard the assets controlled by the system. The trade-offs should not jeopardize the level of control. Using the decision tree, you should be able to describe the needed controls. Using the guidelines and techniques presented in this chapter, you should be able to build the controls into your systems effectively.

8 | Modeling Controls During the Implementation Phase

In the terminology of structured systems development, the implementation phase of the development life cycle consists of coding (programming) and integration testing. It begins with a design specification and ends with a fully tested system, ready for acceptance testing.

But since this isn't a book about how to develop systems, I'm not going to talk about programming. At this point in the life cycle, the controls should have been developed and inserted in the detailed specifications either during the analysis phase or the design phase. The precise way that these controls are implemented is a function of the programming language used, the use of systems like CICS or IMS or similar tools, installation standards, and personal programming style. Each of these has an effect on just how the controls are finally constructed.

Developers may need to introduce new controls during implementation, depending on the particular combination of languages and tools. For example, if a database management system is used, there is a need to build controls into the modules to assure that the DBMS returns the proper codes to indicate successful completion of requested functions. Controls must also assure that if the expected return codes are not received, the system will take appropriate action (for example, oy backing out previously posted parts of a multi-part transaction, or producing the proper error reports). These controls are directly related to decisions made during the technical implementation of *any* system, structured or unstructured. Don't forget them!

In addition to the issue of technical controls internal to the program code being written, there are five control issues that are of concern during the implementation phase: operations controls, input/output control documentation, user documentation, quality assurance, and system testing. They will be discussed in the following sections.

8.1 Operations controls

For years, systems developers have not been taken to task for inadequate operations documentation. I've seen systems that have run in test mode for years, and have thus avoided the documentation standards imposed by the operations people on operational systems. I've also seen systems with operations documentation that has ignored internal control. For example, such documentation may nowhere contain a prohibition against the operator's bypassing label errors. Run-to-run controls often receive short shrift in documentation, too.

The only way to insure that operations documentation effectively describes controls is to review the control provisions decided upon during analysis and design to determine which ones should be reflected in the operations documentation. If the operator can affect the operation of a control, then the control must appear in the documentation.

New controls may be needed to insure that operator mistakes cannot cause serious damage. The need for such controls can be determined only by carefully analyzing all possible interactions between the application system and the operator. For each interaction (loading a file, comparing control totals, and responding to system- or application-generated error messages and requests, for example), consider the range of alternatives available to the operator, and the consequences of making various kinds of errors.

In some cases, this analysis will force you to re-analyze or re-design parts of the system; you may find that you want to build new automated controls. For example, if you discover that the operator can easily mount the wrong tape and override the system-generated warnings, you may want to implement some sort of test within your application program to insure that the file is the correct one. Such a test can easily be designed so that the operator cannot override it.

Similarly, if your programs require the operator to check manually that the system is in balance before initiating follow-up processing steps, you must assess the possibility that the operator won't make the check, or that it will be made incorrectly. If the potential for error appears to be too high, you may wish to substitute an automated test that is difficult or, for all practical purposes, impossible to bypass.

The operations manager and staff and the users can be of great help to the developers in making these determinations. They can often predict whether planned interactions between the operator and the application system are within the range of the operator's abilities, or whether the pressures of the workload are likely to result in control checks being skipped.

8.2 Input/output control documentation

In many organizations, a so-called I/O control group exists independently of the computer operators. Its job is to insure that the applications receive the proper input, and that the output produced is correct and of sufficient quality to release to the system's users. The I/O control specialists need comprehensive, easy-to-understand, and easy-to-use procedures to guide their work. They must know, in detail, what constitutes an error or an out-of-balance condition. For each potential problem identified, clear rules are required for correcting the errors encountered or at least reporting them to the appropriate management level.

The procedure for assessing the effectiveness of I/O control functions is much like that for assessing operations functions. You should analyze the tasks that you plan to assign to the I/O control group. Seek input from operations management, from users, and from the I/O control group. Your job is to determine if the tasks that you proposed are likely to be properly performed. It may turn out that they will probably result in problems; for example, there may be insufficient time to perform the planned I/O control work. If so, go back and modify the plan until you develop one that *will* work.

8.3 User documentation

A major problem in data processing is that systems developers hold the task of developing user documentation in low regard. While there is no doubt of the need for well-written, easy-to-understand user documentation, there is a strong tendency to let the development of the user manuals slip until the very end of a project. Indeed, many systems go into operation without complete user documentation, and some systems have scarcely any. The production of user guides is typically seen as a boring task, unworthy of a highly paid, technically sophisticated systems development professional.

Of course, nothing could be further from the truth. User documentation is often the difference between a successful system and a total failure. When you consider that the whole objective of systems development is to produce a system that meets the user's requirements as well as a system that functions properly, user documentation should be seen as being of equal importance to the automated systems specification. But since documentation is usually neglected, it is imperative to determine during the implementation phase whether the manual controls assigned to the user during development are actually reflected in the user documentation. As you did for operations documentation, document any control whose operation the user can affect.

Keep in mind that most problems in operational systems are traceable to honest errors and omissions made by system users. As a result, you will want your system to be as errorproof as possible, even if it means converting manual controls to automated ones. Clearly, this conversion of controls should be determined as early in development as possible. For that reason, my overall recommendation with regard to manual controls, whether intended for use by operators, I/O control specialists, or users, is this: Prepare initial drafts of manual controls throughout the development process and analyze their feasibility frequently thereafter.

This process is analogous to that discussed above for I/O controls. You plan your controls; verify them through reviews with users and management; verify the operability of the controls through tests where you can; and make whatever modifications are necessary to get the best overall workable set of controls. Then, make sure — again by review and test — that your documentation properly reflects the controls you want and the way that you want them to work. Don't wait until the end. If these decisions are delayed, the increased pressures late in a project may lead to a decision to accept controls known to be impractical. Obviously, this is never a good idea.

8.4 Quality assurance

During the implementation phase, the controls that have been specified for the automated system are given physical existence in the form of code. So during implementation, we have to assure that all of the controls in the design are properly coded, and that all controls are tested. A number of techniques have evolved to do this, key among them being walkthroughs and systems testing.

As you probably know, a walkthrough is a peer-group review of any product. The key to its success is that when rigorously applied a walkthrough assures that every piece of a system is seen by someone (generally more than one person) other than the original author. If you have ever written a report and gone back to read it after a day or so, you know the importance of review. People make mistakes. The best way to catch them is to look for them, and the best way to look for them is with an organized program of reviews.

While walkthroughs have traditionally been associated primarily with reviews of code, they should be applied to every activity in a project right from initial analysis. Four objectives most often set for walkthroughs are *controlling quality* (knowing your work is going to be reviewed by your colleagues motivates you to do a better job); *detecting errors; training* (by participating in walkthroughs of the work of senior people, staff members learn new techniques); and *enforcing standards*.

I suggest that you establish a fifth objective for walkthroughs: *insuring controls*. The walkthrough team should also consider whether the product under review has adequate internal controls to detect and report problems during processing.

8.4.1 The walkthrough process

Let's briefly review the walkthrough process.* The underlying philosophy of a walkthrough is that it is a review of a *product*, not of the *producer* of the product. To be honest, I have trouble accepting that premise. If a group of people denigrate, decimate, reject, and vilify a program that they all know that I did, isn't it human nature to take that as a criticism of me? I think it is. The recognition that one could be made to look foolish in front of one's colleagues gives the walkthrough process its real power. People will work harder and will do a better job in order to avoid embarrassment. So, a powerful psychological force is acting to make walkthroughs effective, to motivate developers of products to build better products. The following guidelines, which are based on my experience, help assure maximum effectiveness of the walkthrough review process.

You need a coordinator to schedule and organize walkthroughs. Particularly on a large project, a lot of products may need to be reviewed, and a significant clerical effort is involved to find walkthrough participants, schedule conference rooms, and distribute materials. Since the work won't get done by itself, this is an excellent job to assign to a paraprofessional employee — such as a program librarian or administrative assistant.

Materials for the walkthrough should be distributed at least two days in advance. In order to keep the actual walkthrough meeting brief and productive, the participants must have ample opportunity to review the materials before the meeting. If the reviewers don't review the material ahead of time, you will not have a successful walkthrough. There is nothing sadder than to see a group of people trying to critique something they haven't seen before. At best, they do a haphazard job.

There seem to be two philosophies about prereview of materials. In one, the review is regarded as an important part of the job, and time is budgeted during the workday for this purpose. In the other, the participants are expected to review the material on their own time. The

---

*Various types of walkthroughs were discussed in Chapter 3; here we concentrate on the process by which walkthroughs are carried out. The discussion is based on E. Yourdon's *Structured Walkthroughs*, 2nd ed. (New York: Yourdon Press, 1978).

drawback of this approach is that the prereview never gets done. If walkthroughs aren't important enough to devote time to during the workday, don't do them, because poor walkthroughs are dangerous. They can give a false sense of security.

A scribe is appointed to take notes during the walkthrough. The set of criticisms generated during a session are the key to the success of walkthroughs. While no one likes being assigned the job of writing down these criticisms, someone has to keep a record during the session so that all criticisms can be addressed.

Walkthroughs can begin with a brief presentation by the author, but that is a waste of everyone's time. If everyone has studied the distributed material, and if the material is complete, what is the author going to say? The material ought to stand on its own.

The coordinator should ask each reviewer, in turn, for comments. Various issues, criticisms, and suggestions are raised and recorded, but are usually not resolved during the walkthrough itself. There should be no arguments, and the coordinator should cut off discussion on any point raised as soon as the participants clearly understand the point. The object is not to have a group debugging session or to rewrite code.

There is a strict time limit for the walkthrough, generally from thirty to sixty minutes. My own vote is for a thirty-minute limit. After all, everyone has reviewed the material before the meeting, and the meeting itself is limited to raising criticisms. If thirty minutes have gone by, and participants are *still* raising criticisms, what are the odds that anyone wouldn't vote to reject the product? Once a negative vote is obvious, how much value is there in continuing the walkthrough?

After all issues have been raised, the coordinator asks for a final vote, which in most organizations can indicate any of the following actions: vote to accept the product as is; vote to accept it, subject to certain revisions that the author is trusted to make without the need to walk through the revised material; or vote to reject it and to require the author to submit the corrected product for another walkthrough.

8.4.2 Taking walkthroughs seriously

One problem of walkthroughs is that participants don't always take them seriously. After all, why should a person vote down a product developed by a friend? This clearly is a management problem. One possible solution is, if a program fails at night, not only is the author called in to fix the error, but all those who approved the product during the walkthrough are called in, too.

The written report of the walkthrough is divided into two parts. The private part of the report, consisting of the detailed findings and criticisms, is given only to the author of the product that was reviewed.

The public part of the report, consisting of a list of walkthrough participants, the identity of the product reviewed, and the final result of the
walkthrough, is filed with the project manager.

8.4.3 The manager's role in walkthroughs

The project manager doesn't attend walkthroughs, because it is
important to keep walkthroughs as peer reviews. Having one's boss at
the walkthrough is intimidating and, therefore, counterproductive.
Nevertheless, some people who disagree voice the following argument:
On some projects, the project manager develops products. Since the
manager's products are subject to walkthroughs, would it not be equit-
able to permit him to participate in the walkthroughs of others? I think
not. The presence of a manager inhibits the other participants. If the
manager insists that fairness requires him to participate, his motives
may be questionable. Perhaps he is out for revenge. One way to avoid
this dilemma is for project managers to walk through each other's work.

The project manager has two important responsibilities with regard to walkthroughs. First, the manager specifies the *products* that will
be subject to walkthroughs. Walkthroughs should be employed
throughout a project and not be limited to reviews of code. There is
great value to be gained from walkthroughs at the analysis and design
phases of the project. The project manager must also set the criteria for
the walkthroughs. That is, he must tell the walkthrough teams the
questions that they must ask during a review. Specifically, he should
consider internal control as part of the walkthrough process, particularly
during analysis- and design-phase walkthroughs.

Finally, the management must allow for walkthroughs in the project schedule. The overhead for a comprehensive walkthrough program
is generally about ten percent. Almost without exception, project
managers have found that the investment is well worth it. Many organizations using walkthroughs report that after the program is underway,
the rejection rate for products drops to one or two percent.

8.5 Systems testing

Many strategies and techniques are used to test systems, each
with its benefits and problems. From an auditing viewpoint, the key requirement is that the testing procedures adequately exercise the controls under all conditions to insure that they work as anticipated. This
is not a trivial undertaking. Developers tend to assume that basic controls work, and to limit testing to exercise the more specialized controls. Every control deserves to be tested and no control should be relied upon until it is in fact tested.

I challenge you to test all of your systems controls. If they work, it should give both the developer and the user confidence in the system. If one or more fail, as often happens, it should prove the need for the testing of all controls. It is far better to discover an error during testing than to discover a malfunctioning control when the system is in operation.

8.6 Conclusion

If you have applied the principles of phase-related control throughout the analysis, design, and implementation phases, your system should be reasonably well controlled. But there are several special issues relating to control that we have not yet covered: reviews of systems documentation and controls over the maintenance process. These will be covered in the following two chapters.

9 | Documentation Reviews

There are documentation reviews, and then again, there are documentation reviews. If I asked you to review the documentation of a systems development project that had just completed the analysis phase, for instance, you wouldn't expect to find the same things as if you were to review an operational system. Obviously, you wouldn't expect to find design and programming documentation before the design and programming phases of the systems development process had been performed.

Regardless of when in the systems development life cycle reviews occur, documentation is a target of auditors' attention. Have you ever noticed that auditors seem to love to do reviews of documentation? I always wondered why they liked them so much. Then, I became an EDP auditor and found out.

9.1 An EDP auditor's mea culpa

Particularly when I was starting out in the auditing field, documentation reviews were something I looked forward to, because they were easy. I had a standard checklist, which told me exactly what to look for: Taking a sample of the documentation, I compared it to the list. Whatever was missing was considered a weakness. As long as I was dealing with a reasonably sized installation, I used the list, and the decisions were generally easy, because I had to select one of only two choices — something was either present or it wasn't.

Looking back, I don't think that was a good way to conduct a review for these three reasons: First, *there are many ways to document a system.* It's unreasonable to hold that *my* particular view of documentation is right, while everyone else's view is wrong. For example, what if I believed that the tools of structured analysis could not provide adequate documentation? While I can state my opinion, I think it unreasonable to treat a matter of opinion as if it were a definitive statement of fact.

My second reason is that *not all systems are the same.* Should you really expect the same sort of documentation for your one-shot reporting program as for the company's payroll or general ledger systems? How much documenting can you do before putting an emergency fix into your system in the middle of the night? (I'll have much more to convey about this in Chapter 10.)

Third, *it's easy to forget that the measure of documentation is usability.* Good documentation enables us to determine what the system does, and how it does it. To evaluate the quality of documentation based on criteria other than pure usability is unreasonable. Consider the issue of whether handwritten documentation is as acceptable as typed documentation. Many of my fellow auditors argue that handwritten documentation isn't as "professional" as typed documentation. I strongly disagree. If documentation is neat, complete, and readable — that is, if it is *usable* — then it should be accepted.

9.2 Structured analysis documentation

First, let's focus on the analysis documentation. If you're the auditor, which of the models in Figure 9.1 should you *insist* be in the documentation? It all depends on the objective of your audit.

Remember that, as the auditor, you can't assume that you know anything about the system that isn't in the documentation. One of the uses of documentation is to serve as a backup tool for the developers and maintainers. If a model is adequate, someone other than the model builder should be able to understand it and to take over development or maintenance, if necessary. By requiring that all information they need about the system appears in the documentation, auditors make sure that the model is an adequate backup tool.

What constitutes adequate documentation of any analysis model considered on a stand-alone basis? The answer to this is clearly defined in the literature of structured analysis: An analysis model is an integrated set of data flow diagrams, a data dictionary, and minispecifications, and may also contain data structure diagrams. Together, they answer the basic question that an analysis model is supposed to answer: What does (or will) the system do?

If I simply gave you a set of data flow diagrams, you would understand quite a lot about the system. You would be able to see the major processes on high-level DFDs and the minor processes on lower-level DFDs. You also could name the dataflows that connect the processes, and you could identify the external sources of data needed by the system and the external destinations of data created by the system.

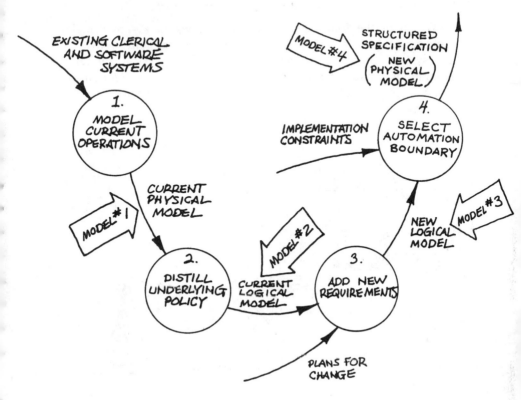

Figure 9.1. The four models in structured analysis.

The ability to derive so much information from a graphic tool like a DFD is the measure of its strength as a modeling tool. But it can't tell you the makeup of dataflows, or the details of the processes operating inside the bottom-level bubbles of the DFDs. If you are conducting a review of a model, you must know those things. The data dictionary and the minispecifications supply that information. So, when we talk about documentation of a model, we're talking about the complete set of tools.

System documentation needs multiple reviews. Let's focus on the possible types of reviews that require examining the documentation of the analysis phase. We will consider the following three reviews: a review of a fully operational system, a review of the internal controls of a system conducted at the end of the analysis phase, and a review of the process by which the system under development was analyzed. For each case, pretend you're the auditor and decide what you would expect to find in the way of documentation.

9.2.1 Operational system documentation review

Which of the four types of models shown in Figure 9.1 should you expect to find in a review of an operational system? Any operational system must be supported by a new physical model, the equivalent of the "as built" specifications for a house. (As shown in Figure 9.2, there is often a significant difference between the plan and its execution.)

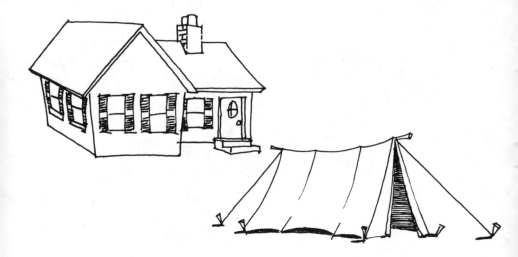

Figure 9.2. Differences between plan and reality.

The distinction between plan and reality is important. The auditor frequently bases an audit plan on the description of the planned system. If the "as built" system differs substantively, the audit plan may turn out to be invalid. In the best of all possible worlds, the auditor wouldn't have to develop the audit plan until the system was developed. In the real world, however, the auditor is forced to build the audit plan when time is available, trusting either that the system will be built as planned, or that if it isn't, the audit testing will discover the differences and the auditor will realize that the tests are invalid.

In addition to the new physical model, should you now expect to find a current logical model? You could argue that it is the physical system that's built, but one of the major purposes of documentation is to make the system *maintainable*. According to the principles of structured analysis, the key to success in maintenance is the use of the logical model to isolate the changes to be made. Further, the logical model gives us a basis for understanding the system regardless of the particular technology to be used. Thus, it makes it feasible to transfer the system between different hardware and software environments. If I were reviewing an operational system built using structured analysis, I would want to see a current logical model.

Should you also expect to find the old logical or old physical models? Remember, you are reviewing the new operational system, not the old system that was replaced. Certainly, there are cases in which having descriptions of the old system would help. (For example, knowing how the prior system was controlled would help generate questions about controls in the new system.) But you've got to separate those things that would perhaps be only nice to have from those that are truly required.

I've written this section from the viewpoint of the auditor. However, consider the problem from the viewpoint of the DP professional who's being audited. How would you feel about being asked to produce the documentation of a system that went out of operation five years ago, and then being criticized for not keeping it? As an auditor, I'm not convinced that it is reasonable to make a fuss when the documentation of the new system doesn't contain documentation of some prior system. (I didn't realize how inappropriate it could be until I challenged a client and insisted that I be shown the documentation for a prior version of the system that I was reviewing. The client took me to the basement of the office building, and into a musty room. He handed me a large, very dusty plugboard from an IBM 407 accounting machine, and said, "Enjoy yourself, Ace!")

9.2.2 Control documentation review at analysis-phase end

At the end of the analysis phase when the target specification has been completed, a review of the documentation is wise. The purpose of the review is to answer the question, Would the system implementing the target specification be well controlled?

That question cannot be answered in full at analysis-phase end because not all the controls are put into a system during the analysis phase. As indicated in Chapter 5, phase-related control shows us that the analysis-time controls alone are insufficient to insure that the implemented system will have comprehensive controls. Design-time and implementation-time controls are of equal import. (After all, computers execute code, not DFDs.) Furthermore, the controls in the analysis documentation have not taken final form. The controls for the automated part of the system must be brought into design and implementation, and the controls in the non-automated portions carried forward into the manual procedures writing process. The controls identified in the analysis phase should be thought of as potential controls.

In spite of their incompleteness, the analysis controls review is important, and to delay it is to risk incurring the significant expense associated with retrofitting controls later in the systems development process. But recognize that whatever type of review of the documentation is performed at the end of the analysis phase, the review isn't really of the total set of systems controls. I stress this point because it's easy to fool yourself into believing that you are doing more than you really are.

So, what should you look for at the end of analysis? Clearly, you will want to review the new physical model, since it represents the system components (both manual and automated) to be sent along for design and implementation. You'll also probably want to look at the new logical model to assist you in understanding the business functions that underlie the implementation details inherent in the new model. Do you want to see the documentation of the current system? I, for one, would certainly like to, although, as I said before, it may be unnecessary in some cases. Since basic business processes supported by our systems tend to change slowly, the new system will probably perform most of the functions that the present system does (although it may do so in a different way). If I could understand the controls in the old system, I'd have a reasonable basis for beginning an analysis of controls in the new system.

Of course, even if I had good documentation of the old system, which experience shows is not highly likely, it wouldn't be enough. One reason is that while the new system will have many functions in common with the old system, only in the rarest cases will there be a one-to-one mapping of functions. The new and changed functions must be supported with appropriate controls, and you can't expect to find these in an old system description. A second reason that documentation of the old system is insufficient is that the old system's controls may not have been good or even adequate — if they were ever consciously considered. Hence, they could be a poor model on which to base the new system's controls. It is far more useful to know whatever we can about the shortcomings in the controls of the present system. Now, where might you look for such statements of shortcomings? The answer will differ for each organization, but some starting points for your search include the management letter, prepared by your organization's external auditors; various internal audit reports; problems in the present system documented during the feasibility study (survey) phase of the systems development process; and interviews with users and internal auditors.

The above discussion should give you the impression that a review of systems controls documentation at the end of the analysis phase doesn't tell you whether the system that was defined is the right system. The review's objective is to determine whether the planned controls make sense.

What if you were charged with determining whether the analysis team did a good job of determining systems requirements? What would you look for? The next section addresses these questions.

9.2.3 Documentation reviews of the systems analysis process

One of the major tasks performed by data processing quality assurance personnel, as well as many DP professionals, is to review the process by which the analysis of the system was performed. What specifically would such a review focus on?

First and most important, the reviewer of the analysis process must verify that every part of the system receives enough attention from the analyst. Consider that any computerized system can be viewed as being composed of several concentric circles (see Figure 9.3). Observation of systems analysts' work shows us that they have a strong tendency to concentrate their attention on the innermost circle — the computerized portions of the system. Analysts show a genuine lack of interest in spending much time worrying about the details of the manual procedures. In light of the disasters that have resulted from systems being implemented without adequate manual procedures, it is amazing that management permits this problem to continue unabated. The data processing landscape is littered with great automated systems that utterly failed, because no one built the manual procedures and controls necessary to drive the computer programs.

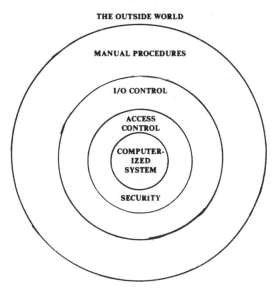

Figure 9.3. Layers of system protection.

I don't think that I'm going out on a thin limb when I tell you that the problem of inadequate manual procedures is going to continue.* I urge you to challenge your ideas of what constitutes good documentation of the systems analysis process. You should not accept documentation of the computerized portion of any system as being all that is required.

Traditional documentation makes the failure to provide adequate manual procedures documentation almost inevitable. Consider the tools that we used before we learned about the tools of structured analysis. Primarily, traditional analysis specifications ("functional specifications") were built using tools considered appropriate for describing a computerized function. The system builders believed that narratives and flowcharts were the *ne plus ultra* of systems analysis. These linear tools ("do this, then do this, then do that") were in fact a pretty good way to describe the flows of control that exist within a program module. But usefulness of linear tools for function description doesn't extend to non-linear processes, such as entire systems. In fact, the use of the wrong tools for the analysis process leads to severe problems.

Because tools can have an important effect on the quality of the analysis product, the reviewer of the systems analysis process needs to evaluate them carefully. To show you what a reviewer should look for, I discuss below four problems caused by using poor tools. The reviewer should examine the tools used by the project under investigation to determine how well they succeed in avoiding these problems.

The first is what are referred to as *Victorian novels.*† I once gave a fisherman's combination scale and tape measure neatly labeled as a "module meter" to a former boss of mine. It was the perfect gift, because his criterion for excellence of a systems analysis effort was the physical size of the resulting specification. The problems with Victorian novel specs are obvious: First, they are endless. Second, they are often

---

*If you want to know why I feel confident of this, look in the DP Help Wanted advertisements to compare the relative salary levels of DP and manual systems analysts. Then, compare them with your knowledge of salaries in any good-sized DP organization with which you've ever been associated. If there were any manual systems analysts, where did they stand in the prestige pecking order? Pretty far down, right? As long as manual systems analysis is held in low regard, DP systems analysts won't perceive it as a terrific way to spend their time.

†Tom DeMarco, author of *Structured Analysis and System Specification* (New York: Yourdon Press, 1978), points out that a manager who judged the quality of analysis by the weight or thickness of documentation guaranteed a specification that had several characteristics in common with Victorian novels.

almost impossible to read without falling asleep. Of course, the major failing of this kind of specification is that there is no effective way of being sure that it contains all necessary functions, that it contains no unnecessary functions, that the necessary functions are described properly, and that the specification is not redundant. Perhaps the most critical failing is that the more complex and lengthy a specification, the less likely it is that it will be reviewed completely or competently.

A second severe problem of using inadequate or inappropriate analysis tools is that they produce *poor models*. While Victorian novels are almost guaranteed to be unreviewable, even in those cases when a smaller specification is produced, there is no guarantee of quality. A bad model — one that doesn't reflect what the system actually does (in the case of current system models) or one that suggests a system that won't meet its objectives (in the case of new system models) — is worse than none at all. If you don't have a model, obviously you know that you don't have one. But if you have any model, it's tempting and all too easy to simply accept it, and proceed with design. Resist temptation, and ask yourself a few questions before you accept any analysis model: How do you know it's a reasonable model? Who has reviewed it? users? How thorough do you think they really were in their review? What process did the analysts use to develop the model? Whom did they talk to? Did they schedule feedback sessions with the key information sources? (Answers to many of these questions should be available in project control documentation.)

The third and most common problem caused by applying incorrect tools is the development of *specifications that are not user oriented.* Incorrect tools allow developers to describe solutions without ever having described the problem. Therefore, the solution may reflect the developer's prejudices instead of the user's needs. A common delusion is that a specification must specify a data processing solution to whatever problem is presented. Some systems analysts don't or won't admit that a computerized solution may not be required. They define the problem in such a way as to justify a computer-based solution. (This is what the old saying "If the only tool you have is a hammer, every problem looks a lot like a nail" is all about.) What's worse is that the specification is written in a way that is inconvenient for users to review. For example, look at the DFD in Figure 9.4.

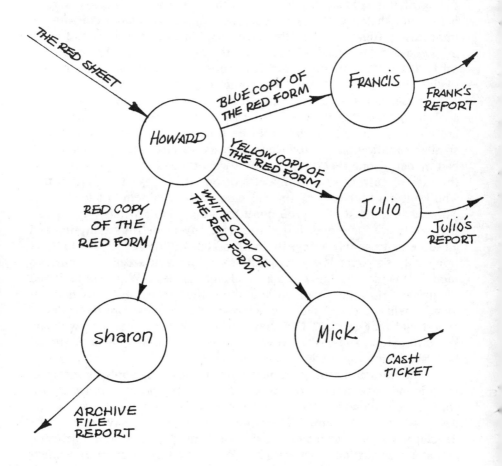

Figure 9.4. A physical DFD.

As you can see, Figure 9.4 is quite physical. It has people's names and commonly used names for forms. A user could verify that this is indeed what happens in his organization today. Even if we logicalize the diagram, it is still verifiable (see Figure 9.5).

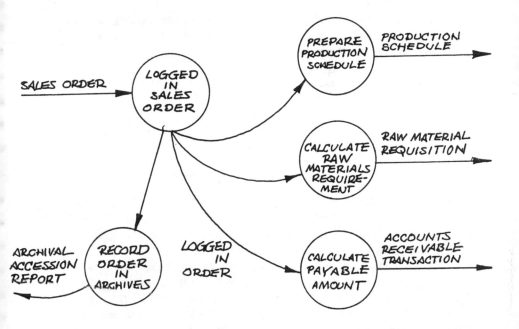

Figure 9.5. Logical version of the Figure 9.4 DFD.

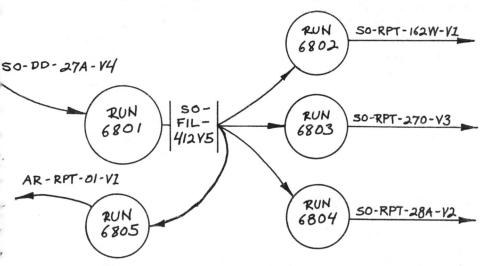

Figure 9.6. A technician's view of the Figure 9.4 DFD.

Now look at one DP technician's view of the same process (Figure 9.6). The technician has diagrammed a current system by giving run numbers for the process names and data dictionary entry serial numbers for the dataflow names. This view of a system is incomprehensible to a user.

An even more common problem concerns the naming of data. If you were a user, which of the following lists of data names would you be most likely to understand?

User's View	Forms Control's View	Technician's View
Salesman's Commission Report	R6-59UL-V7	S.68.COMRPT.01
Translator's Work Schedule	Q7-G602-9/82	V.68.TWS.VO1.SCHED
Sales Tax Collection Report	LNGFORM 861	ST-COL-RPT-TRANS-RCD
Occupational Analysis File	84694132841	OA-MF-O1-V1

Figure 9.7. Three views of data.

Granted, in Figure 9.7, the list on the right is fancier, and probably meets installation standards for naming data. However, in forming this list the analyst forgot that the purpose of analysis is problem definition, not the detailing of a particular data processing solution.

The fourth problem of using the wrong analysis tools is the *premature assumption of solutions.* Analysts have an almost uncontrollable desire to develop solutions. Almost as soon as they begin to define a problem, the analysts begin to block out a solution and, in effect, quickly begin to define a man-machine boundary. Their tendency then is to concentrate on the automated portion of the system. As you know from previous chapters, a principle of structured analysis is to avoid setting the automation boundary until the entire problem is defined and understood. Typically, this boundary is set during the transition from the new logical to the new physical model. If the boundary is set before this point, proceed with the greatest of care, because it will be impossible to determine whether the proposed solution is based on the problem and the user's needs, or on the analyst's desires. The easiest way to detect this bias is by reviewing the analysis documentation to determine whether the manual portions of the overall system were given short shrift. Although no one involved in the analysis will appreciate your pointing out their failings, that's your job as a reviewer.

As I've emphasized in the previous chapters, it's a lot better to have this kind of problem pointed out in the analysis phase than to have it noticed when the system is set for installation. A DP department with a history of failed acceptance tests, or with a consistent pattern of having many enhancements to newly installed systems, should be suspect. The only way that these problems can occur regularly is if management allows it.

9.3 Structured design documentation

Once we've decided *what* our new system is to do, structured design can help us to develop and to document the architecture and detailed processing of the automated portions of the new system. What constitutes reasonable documentation of the structured design? There is no single answer, as organizations use different techniques to reach the same objective. Since all of the various techniques are quite reasonable and defensible, the reviewer must apply judgment based upon knowledge in order to judge the quality of structured design documentation.

9.3.1 Documentation of structured design

In reviewing structured design documentation, one must try to gain a clear understanding of how the physical pieces of a system — generally modules — fit together. The system may be documented in many ways, including with flowcharts, HIPO diagrams, and structure charts.* While a technical discussion of these tools would be out of place in this book, the structure chart offers a number of advantages to the reviewer, of which two are worth noting here.

First, the structure chart permits direct charting of module-to-module calls, wherein one module orders another module to execute and, following execution, to return control to the calling module. The structure chart shows the data exchanged between the calling and called modules in both directions. Flowcharts are not designed to show call relationships. HIPO charts, in my opinion, show the information in a more complex way than do structure charts. Second, the structure chart indicates the data and control information passed between modules. If the data necessary to properly control the system is not present, that fact is obvious.

9.3.2 Documentation of the procedural design

There are a number of ways that systems developers may choose to document procedural design. By procedural design, I mean the description of *exactly* what each part (module) in a system does. The auditor is less interested in the exact technique used than in how well the objective of clear, concise, unambiguous description is met.[†]

---

*For more information on these tools, see E. Yourdon's *Managing the Structured Techniques,* 2nd ed. (New York: Yourdon Press, 1979), pp. 74-75.
[†]Ibid, pp. 142-58.

Whether the designer uses narrative, Nassi-Shneiderman diagrams, detailed HIPO charts, decision trees, decision tables, or a combination of these and other tools, the objective is the same: Can a reviewer understand the processes being described? Perhaps the best advice is to let the problem define the tools to be used. Pseudocode is often a preferred solution, since it is easy to produce and uses the tools of structured programming (constructs such as sequence, iteration, and decision) to express procedural details. Where multiple decisions are involved, decision trees or tables can be put to good use. Again, the reviewer should concentrate on understandability rather than dwelling on personal beliefs about specific forms of documentation.

9.4 The bottom-line decision

Now, let's assume that you've been given a model of a proposed new system that has been built with reasonable tools, that has considered the whole system (both manual and automated portions), and that does not suffer from the ills described in Section 9.2. Shall we give the analysis and design processes a clean bill of health? The answer must be that *we have insufficient data on which to base a decision.* Why? Because it is possible (perhaps even easy) to build a magnificent specification for the wrong system. I could do it without ever leaving my desk and without ever speaking to the users.

The point of all this, patient reader, is to build a case for the following assertion: *The objective of systems development is not to produce proper documentation; it is to produce proper systems* (which we pray will be properly documented). Reviewing the process requires more than a review of the final documentation. It requires a review of the project management documentation. Who was interviewed? for what purposes? In what detail was the old system studied? how? for how long? Who signed off on what?

This can get to be a long list of questions; and project management is somewhat outside the scope of this book. Therefore, after almost nine chapters of a book on controls, I want to make a few short statements to remind you that the documentation that you produce or review must contain all the controls that we have discussed. If you can't find the controls in the documentation, there is only one reasonable assumption — the controls aren't there!

Remember as well that from final documentation you can tell a great deal about a project, but not everything. If I were told to review the analysis process, for example, I would be out there with the users asking for their view of the process, and I would spend considerable time interviewing the project director and staff to explore how they did the work and why they chose to do it as they did.

This chapter is rapidly drawing to a close and I have neither included any definitive checklists nor referred you to an appendix. You are undoubtedly asking, "How could Brill do this to us? If structured stuff is so darn structured, why couldn't he come up with a few lousy checklists? Lazy bum!"

The "oversight" is intentional. Since you understand structured analysis, design, and programming, you know that the developers of those disciplines never intended their work to be graven into stone tablets. I'm not about to pick up the hammer and chisel, because they were right. A checklist makes things *too* easy. It doesn't induce you to think about your audit, or about the system that you are reviewing. Your knowledge of the structured techniques, along with the issues raised in this chapter and elsewhere in this book, should give you the ammunition that you need to develop customized audit plans for any system and any situation.

10 | Maintenance Reviews

Let's talk about maintenance. Almost no one in data processing likes to do maintenance. I never did, and I'll bet you don't either. Maybe the reason is that there seems to be an endless supply of it. I'll spare you all the statistics about maintenance consuming 50 percent of data processing budgets, or representing 80 percent of systems lifetime costs, or the federal government's spending about $1.3 billion on software maintenance in the 1979-1980 fiscal year. The reason that auditors show such an interest in systems maintenance is that it accounts for so much of data processing's total resources, and it seems to foul up as many systems as it repairs.

The statistics are nothing more than dry figures. Doubtless your personal experience tells you more than do statistics about the amount of maintenance that can exist in even a small shop. What I want to suggest in this chapter is that maintenance is so painful because we traditionally haven't built our systems to be maintainable.

Also remember that not all maintenance activities are the same. Ongoing debugging is *very* different from changes required by new hardware or new operating systems, and that type of maintenance is very different from that caused by user-requested changes or enhancements to an application.

10.1 Building maintainable systems

In most systems development projects, the problems that seem important include these: how to get something (anything!) up and running by the delivery date, how to get computer operations to accept responsibility for running the system, how to convince the user that he really wants the system that you're set to deliver, and how to survive being involved with this disastrous project.

When you're building a system, of course, you never expect that *you* will have to maintain the monster you're creating. So why worry about something in the future (like maintenance) when the present is terrifying enough?

The problem is well described by Meilir Page-Jones:*

> The overriding consideration of system developers is to deliver a system by the deadline and within the budget. Judging from the times I've seen system testing hastily drawn to a premature close because of the impending due date, I would say that delivering a *working* system is a secondary consideration. Well down on the list — and seldom even considered — is delivering a flexible system. If the system works at all, that's often regarded as a miracle. Future changes are scarcely given a thought.
>
> However, barely is the system in production when an unexpected avalanche of changes will rumble down from the user onto the poor development team, who are still patting themselves on the back over the "success" of this latest system. Usually the system, only just hanging together in the first place, cannot absorb these changes gracefully. Many systems lose their dubious stability early in their lifetime: After a few months, they never again function completely correctly.
>
> Trying to incorporate quite reasonable user changes after development is even more frustrating and costly than it is during the development effort. I know of one very large system that is currently occupying the full-time attention of more than one hundred maintenance programmers. These lost souls are organized into six-person chain gangs (their term, not mine). Each chain gang is responsible for one set of features, aspects, or functions of the system. Whenever a problem arises in a particular part of the system, the appropriate chain gang shuffles off to eliminate the offending bugs. Unfortunately, this approach, while good in theory, doesn't work well in practice. Too often, when one gang makes a change to its part of the system, a part belonging to a very different gang stops working correctly. So that gang shuffles over to make *its* corrections. This fix-and-shuffle routine is almost non-stop. The system wobbles along, barely working at all and never working completely. . . .
>
> Why is maintenance so expensive? Because none of the six steps that comprise maintenance is easy. The steps involved in changing a system include

---

*M. Page-Jones, *The Practical Guide to Structured Systems Design* (New York: Yourdon Press, 1980), pp. 30-32.

1. understanding how the current system works (or why it doesn't work)

2. figuring out the required modification

3. assessing the impact of the modification on the rest of the system

4. making the modification

5. testing the modified system

6. managing, organizing, controlling, and documenting the above

Steps 1, 2, and 3 are usually unnecessarily difficult in conventional systems because of the system's lack of design. When the true impact of the lack of design becomes apparent, during maintenance, it's too late to make amends. Correcting the poor design of a system in production is an order of magnitude more expensive than correcting it during design. (Imagine trying to change the plan of an office building *after* it's been built.)

Another major problem making Steps 1, 2, and 3 extremely difficult is the typical lack of high-level documentation for a system. Trying to understand a system from its code alone has been compared to investigating an elephant from a distance of two inches: All you can tell is that it's gray!

Steps 5 and 6 are always tedious and dull. Therefore, in practice, Step 4 is the only one that will definitely be carried out. But without the other steps, a quick succession of Step 4's will soon beat the system into an unmaintainable pulp. (That's especially true if the modifications are carried out over many years by many generations of maintenance programmers. Their diverse prejudices, talents, and levels of experience result in systems with immensely confusing and inconsistent programming styles. Such systems have been called Baskin-Robbins® systems — 31 flavors of code!)

This amounts to saying that with classical systems the six steps of maintenance are far too time-consuming and costly if you do them. And, they're even more time-consuming and costly if you don't!

10.2 The three types of maintenance

As I mentioned earlier, all maintenance isn't the same. From the viewpoint of both the auditor and the data processing staff, there are three major classes of maintenance: ongoing debugging; changes required by new hardware, operating systems, communication systems, and database management systems; and expansions of system capabilities and addition of new features. Let's look at each class below.

10.2.1 Ongoing debugging

Ongoing debugging is the set of actions (usually frantic) that systems developers perform on a delivered operational system in order for it to meet its original functional specification. Put more directly, it is the process of fixing the errors and shortcomings that were in the system (but that you assured the user weren't).

Ongoing maintenance shouldn't happen. It absolutely infuriates users, and rightly so! With all of the ballyhoo, running around, late delivery, over-budget delivery, and magnificent promises that characterize so much of the systems development process, and *particularly* after assurance that thorough testing had been carried out prior to the delivery of the system, it really *ought* to work. And when, as usual, the system doesn't, the user feels trapped. Too much has been invested in the disabled system to scrap it. The time necessary to carry out what the DP people assure the users are "trivial" repairs starts expanding. And expanding.*

Given the total amount of data processing resources spent on this ongoing debugging, the amount of static generated by users, the magnitude of bad feeling generated between DP and users, and, perhaps most of all, given the realization that with all the debugging going on, the assets being controlled or recorded by the system are "at risk," is it a surprise that auditors focus their attention on this area? Of course, their fear is based on the recognition that a "fix" installed in one part of a system could "unfix" something else. ("What do you mean, there isn't any more Accounts Receivable File since you fixed the sales tax table? How can you not know where it went?")

I'm totally unconvinced that there is any way to eliminate ongoing debugging. It is very difficult to produce large amounts of totally bug-free code: As you all are well aware, the chances of completely fixing a bug on the first try aren't very good. Nevertheless, I am convinced that the amount of debugging that accompanies a traditional project is way out of line.

This conviction comes from observing that these ongoing problems seem to exist (in traditionally developed systems) independently of the amount of testing that's performed. Typically, a lot of testing is done. Figures cited in books by Brooks and by Metzger† indicate that

---

*Einstein said that time dilation was only significant at speeds approaching that of light. If he had checked with users, he would have known that time dilation operates at the speed of debugging.
†See F.P. Brooks, Jr., *The Mythical Man-Month* (Reading, Mass.: Addison-Wesley, 1975), and P. Metzger, *Programming Project Management,* 2nd ed. (Englewood Cliffs, N.J.: Prentice-Hall, 1982).

the following pie chart represents the typical distribution of time in a traditional systems development project (see Figure 10.1).

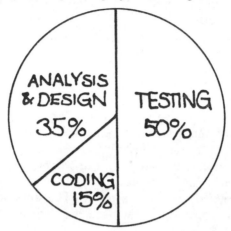

Figure 10.1. Typical project time budget.

Can you imagine spending 50 percent of a project's time testing? (Of course you can; you've been there, and so have I.) After such extensive testing, imagine *still* having months of ongoing debugging to look forward to.

The reason for this is that the activity that we call "testing" isn't really testing. Most of the time is spent reworking inadequate analysis, design, and programming work. Or, quite often, the time is spent actually doing the analysis or design work that wasn't done during the analysis and design phases of the development process.

One of the primary reasons analysis and design are not carried out completely and comprehensively during the initial part of projects is that user management won't allow the necessary time. Data processing professionals are partly to blame because they fail to explain the importance of proper analysis and design and do not point out the economic consequences of inadequate analysis and design. Indeed, where users understand what analysis and design are, and how they help to minimize the cost of systems development, they support the scheduling of sufficient time for analysis and design.

A friend told me years ago that from the viewpoint of most users, there are only two phases to any systems development project. The "program writing" stage is one. Users understand that systems need programs, and can accept DP people devoting time to writing programs. Then there's the period between the start of the project and the start of program writing. Systems developers would use such terms as "feasibility survey," "analysis," and "design" to describe this period. The users often refer to it as the *resting-up phase*. They figure that developers need some time to rest up, to gather strength before getting to the "real work" of coding. As a result, it's often tempting to fold under user pressure to get on with the coding. So programmers start coding, knowing full well that not enough analysis or design has been done. Whether it's ever done is doubtful.

The disciplines of structured analysis and structured design provide a framework to help assure that complete analysis and design are done. However, the problem of ongoing maintenance, which has drawn the attention of quality control and review specialists, won't go away just because we have new tools. Until we can prove — through improved systems development techniques — that we are building systems correctly from the start, rather than relying on high volumes of maintenance to correct flawed analyses and designs, this work will be subject to careful scrutiny by auditors.

10.2.2 *Changes required by new hardware and systems software*

Every time an installation I was once associated with announced that it was going to "upgrade" the hardware, operating system, database management systems, or any other piece of systems software, there was an accompanying announcement that read as follows:

> Systems analysts and application programmers should not concern themselves with these changes in the operating environment. We will see to it that the new systems are totally transparent to the applications.

I was naive (or dumb) enough to believe that assertion once — but never again. The conversion to a new computer, an upgraded version of the operating system, or a new database management system always seemed to be the occasion for putting a mass of unrelated changes into the system.

Now, changes in the operating environment do require some changes to applications on occasion. But shouldn't the changes be localized and severely limited to a few modules? They should but almost never are in practice.

The reason for many of the disorganized activities that accompany new hardware and systems software installation became clear to me once I understood that a dangerous syndrome was present in epidemic proportions in the DP population:

The "Try It, You'll Like It" Syndrome

When data processing people get their hands on hardware or software that has new bells and whistles, there is an irresistible temptation to ring all the bells and sound all the whistles.

The problem is that in order to use the bells and whistles, the system's functions must be changed. For example, to exercise the full power of the latest relational razzle-dazzle database system, the developers are tempted to give users access to more or different data than users ever said they needed.

This tendency is well known to auditors, and gives them fits, because developers usually forget to tell the user about the new capabilities, forget to document exactly what was done, and forget to test everything before putting the revised system into the production libraries.

10.2.3 Expansion of capabilities and new features

Functional changes can usually be divided into two groups. The first includes those enhancements needed to bring a system built on the basis of a frozen specification up-to-date. The second group includes the valid user requests, which may range from truly trivial changes to major system revisions.

The trouble is that sometimes those trivial changes are made in a short time — with no real analytic thought and with limited testing and quality control. Clearly, the users' joy with the changed and new features of their systems is tempered by the bugs that so often accompany them. Bugs are particularly prevalent when the changes are made on a "crash" basis.

In the programmer's defense, what is he going to do when the users give him three hours to change the way employee benefits are calculated? Anyone who tells you that a crisis is no excuse for failing to follow installation programming, quality assurance, or management practices hasn't been there. In such a case, the programmer's only desire in life is to get the change done so that all the people screaming at him will just leave him in peace.

Any auditor who's being honest recognizes the problem of modifying a system on a crash basis. The auditor is justifiably concerned about what happens afterward. Does the programmer try to repress the work as being a bad dream, or does he follow up by reviewing the change, and immediately replacing it with a real enhancement, based on analysis, quality control, and testing?

10.3 Three practices that hinder good maintenance

To summarize, I cite three major reasons that auditors and quality control specialists focus their attention on maintenance work:

- Maintenance represents a large proportion of the DP budget.

- Maintenance represents a large proportion of the total life cycle cost of application systems.

- Many bugs and control weaknesses are introduced during the maintenance process.

In this section, we focus on the last reason. Three syndromes that plague systems maintenance are responsible for the carelessness that allows bugs and control weaknesses into systems during maintenance.

The China Syndrome (EDP Version)

Users believe that DP organizations have 850,000,000 people available to perform maintenance.

From the viewpoint of any individual user, the question of priority is an easy one. The equation is, *My priority is top priority.* If there is only a single user, that works out fine. But when, as in the usual case, there are many users of data processing services, how can everyone have top priority? Obviously everyone can't. Not every problem or request can be handled instantly.

Users often seem incapable of understanding that data processing departments have capacity problems, and that everything cannot be done at once. The problem of ordering priorities has long plagued software maintenance managers, but it doesn't trouble some users. They can build an airtight case to demonstrate why *their* work must be given the absolute top priority. This leads to constant crises, as management tries to maximize total user satisfaction by moving the maintenance jobs through as quickly as possible. When the pressure is on, it's tempting to cut corners by doing quick fixes, rather than performing comprehensive, careful maintenance.

The "Maybe It Will Go Away" Syndrome

Users forget to tell DP managers about forthcoming changes in requirements until the due date arrives.

For example, if a law is scheduled to go into effect six months from now, when will the DP department be informed? Often, not until just before the law goes into effect.

I don't attribute malice to the users. It's easy to assume that someone else is passing information along to the DP people. For example, consider the following Friday afternoon dialogue between a user and a data processing maintenance manager:

USER: We're really looking forward to the revisions in the Credit Scoring System that you're installing on Monday.

DP: Revisions? What revisions are those?

USER: You know. The ones to take care of those revisions in the Fair Credit Access Law.

DP: I don't know what you're talking about.

USER: You guys are great kidders!

DP: No. Really. I don't know what you're talking about.

USER: Sure. You don't know that as of Monday, our current Credit Scoring Algorithm is illegal and that we have to use the formula in the revised law. You techies are a barrel of laughs.

DP: Listen, I don't know anything about any changes in the Credit Scoring System. And the system that you're going to run on Monday is the same as you've got today. Sorry.

USER: Sorry? *You're* going to be more than sorry, Ace. You'll have those changes in by Monday, *or else!*

Sound familiar? It should, because it happens all the time. You know the result as well as I do: crisis! emergency! overtime!

If there's one action that DP staff members can take to reduce aggravation relating to maintenance, it is to set up an early warning system. Communications *must* be established with users in such a way that DP staff learn of changes as far in advance as is possible. In large part, the ability to do this depends upon the users' perceptions of the reactions to their early warning messages. If the messages are met by moans and groans, future warnings are not likely to be sent.

Of course, there's a world of difference between receiving advance notice and taking prompt action, as illustrated by the next syndrome.

The "What? Me Worry?" Syndrome

Even with early notice of changes, DP people develop amnesia until the due date is upon them.

DP staff often complain that they are "forced" to operate in *crisis mode* all the time. Yet all the while they are complaining, they are procrastinating. They frequently fail to take advantage of advance notice of system changes. So they make their own crises. I've heard systems managers boast that they "worked best under pressure." Maybe some of them do, but one thing is clear: When work is done under crisis conditions, controls often take a back seat to mere survival. "How can you expect us to consider controls when we hardly have enough time to get the system up and running?" the harried systems manager cries. "This is a crisis!"

Maybe so, but when it's a crisis of DP's own making, it becomes hard to sympathize.

10.4 What auditors should look for in maintenance reviews

There are five issues that must be considered in any review of the maintenance process. How is maintenance planned and authorized? How is the impact of a change identified? How is it assured that maintenance won't negatively affect controls? How are modifications tested? How is "emergency" maintenance handled? Let's consider each of these.

How is maintenance planned and authorized? In a review of maintenance, the auditor must consider how the process of maintenance is controlled. Is there some formalized (or at least informally ritualized) way to plan maintenance? Is there an early warning system? Is there some way to avoid an unnecessary crisis? Can needless changes be avoided? Are changes monitored to determine when to begin considering re-design or major upgrading of systems, rather than doing endless maintenance?

How is the impact of a change identified? Of course, if the DP installation is using structured methods, the systems maintenance team knows to use the logical and physical data flow diagrams and the structure charts to determine the technical impact of a change, and thus both avoid excess work and reasonably estimate the resources needed to make the change. There's a second issue to be considered: Often, DP staff use maintenance changes as an excuse to make unrequested changes to a system. If anyone hears the following words, "As long as we're going to be rummaging around in that part of the system, we might as well throw in some technical enhancements," watch out! More unrequested, possibly unneeded, and undocumented work is slipped in under the guise of maintenance than you can imagine. Regardless of what the maintenance team is doing, team members must acknowledge their responsibility for the extra work and control it. Simply from a cost accounting viewpoint, I wouldn't want to charge time spent, say, on installing a new database management system to user-requested maintenance. When there is a formalized charge-back system in effect, such actions smack of fraud. What auditors look for in a review is the way in which DP determines how to implement a given change most cost effectively.

How do auditors assure that maintenance won't damage controls? Maintenance actions have often caused the internal controls of applications to deteriorate seriously. In part, this occurs because the controls are built in as afterthoughts and aren't terribly flexible. Indeed, the jury-rigged controls often can't withstand any changes. Even worse, most of the time no one notices that the controls have been deactivated during maintenance and that disaster is imminent. The easiest way to avoid these problems is to review changes in applications to *insure* that the revised system has controls that are at least as strong as those in the current system. Clearly, if this strategy is to work, the need for control has to be a prime consideration in judging the impact of a change. I suggest that the place to begin that consideration is in the user's area. If your DP shop uses a standard form for a maintenance request, why not include a question about controls (such as, "How will the requested change affect the controls?").

How are modifications tested? Endless stacks of material have been written on the need for comprehensive testing of modifications, and I don't want to add to the pile. Let me merely remind you that, in making the tests, it's important to test the controls over the portion of the system that was maintained, *even if it doesn't seem that the controls could have been affected.*

How are emergency maintenance cases handled? Is there any consideration of control, not to the extent that it unduly delays fixing the problem, but at least to the extent that severe problems are prevented? (For example, payroll systems must have controls to keep track of payments made and checks printed. Emergency maintenance cannot be permitted to reduce control below some irreducible kernel.) More important, what follow-up action is taken the morning after? Emergency maintenance activities should be held to the same standards as routine maintenance actions.

10.5 Conclusion

Maintenance is vital. Organizations spend a fortune on it, but with regard to controls, it frequently is the weak link in the chain. Controls can be easily degraded, and the degradation can go unnoticed until something terrible happens.

My recommendation to prevent this degradation is that auditors review their organization's procedures to determine how much (if at all) controls are considered in the maintenance process, and to determine how to make sure controls are considered if they aren't now. The objective, of course, is not to make auditors responsible for building or maintaining the controls, but rather to give the user and the DP professional the primary responsibility for assuring the adequate control of the system.

11 | A Plan for Action

How can you introduce the careful consideration of internal control into your own organization? There are many ways to do so, and I discuss the keys to success in this final chapter. But before I do, I want to warn you of several methods that are certain *not* to work.

11.1 Three plans destined to fail

Over the years, auditors, DP staff, and managers have unsuccessfully tried a number of plans to implement programs similar to our program of control consciousness. I present three examples in the following subsections.

11.1.1 The floating apex approach

In the floating apex approach, a senior manager, either corporate or data processing, takes up the cry of "let's do it" (whatever "it" is). There is no other visible support, and no program for implementing the new program or for training. No one other than the originating senior official feels any commitment to the program. As a result, everyone under the boss's authority determines the least effort to keep the boss happy, and everyone does that minimum for the least amount of time.

What's unfortunate in this approach is that the senior manager often doesn't realize that no one is doing anything. Sure, everyone seems to be in line with the boss's wishes, but it's all lip service. When the lack of commitment becomes apparent to the boss, the boss usually interprets it as a failure of the program. I can hear the excuse now: "That internal control stuff is no good. Everyone tried it, and nothing happened. What a waste of time!"

The lesson is, Don't adopt this approach. A program with only a senior manager behind it is in trouble from the start. Don't undertake a program unless you're prepared to work hard to engender wide support. If the systems developers — the project leaders, analysts, designers, and programmers — won't get behind the program, it won't work and shouldn't be undertaken.

11.1.2 The sputtering blitz approach

A sputtering blitz occurs when a big program is announced to introduce some new idea (like control consciousness), and it isn't followed through. Everyone gets interested and often works hard to succeed, but the lack of follow-through and resources poisons the program. Following the initial period of enchantment, project managers may no longer be given the time to conduct walkthroughs for control. Or, time may not be allowed for use of the control classification tool, for example, for use of the control decision tree discussed in Chapter 4. Or, no one in management seems to care about the state of internal control in systems under development. In essence, the program is just a whim that disappears for lack of interest.

The only way around this problem is to plan a long-term solution to an actual data processing systems problem, and to recognize that there is no necessity for a blitz or huge initial publicity program at all. I have found that the best support for any program is grass-roots support. It's better to explain the problem, demonstrate solutions, and teach people to understand that the subject is of long-term significance to the organization, and hence to them.

11.1.3 The disappearing pilot approach

Sometimes, management decides to try out a program by selecting a pilot project and applying new techniques on it. That can be a terrific approach if the results of the project are applied elsewhere. However, what often happens is that the technique is used in the pilot, and then never again. No one receives any particular credit for participating in the pilot. The techniques are not disseminated to other projects. The pilot-tested techniques just seem to die on the vine.

Why does this happen? Again, it is because of a lack of commitment. A pilot program is sometimes undertaken to give the appearance of action, and it is often a part of the reaction to the floating apex approach. It represents an easy answer to the question, "What are you doing to implement this program?" Any time a pilot program isn't clearly seen to be only a test project, it's going to fail. It's important to have a program laid out to exploit the success of the pilot effort.

Without such a plan, any success in the pilot and any momentum for spreading the new techniques will be lost. If, after a successful pilot test, you ask "What now?" you've wasted your time on the pilot. Don't undertake a pilot test unless you expect that it will succeed. And if you expect it to succeed, then you should have a plan to exploit the pilot's success.

11.2 A plan that can work

In contrast to the three previous examples of failure in introducing internal control awareness, let's now look at a plan to succeed. I divide the factors for success into three groups: those that help a program get started; those that help to build controls into new systems; and those that help to retrofit controls into existing systems during the maintenance process.

11.2.1 Getting started

Whatever the processes that succeed for you in your organization, here are some factors that often are associated with successful introduction of new ideas and techniques. Specifically, they include motivation, necessary training, integration of internal controls into the systems development life cycle, and provisions for walkthroughs and other controls over the process of building controls. I'll briefly discuss each one below.

Motivation seems to be the most important factor for success. To motivate people, you must tell them why internal controls are important, both to the organization, and more important, to themselves. They have to be convinced that what you are proposing to do is neither the reaction to the demands of some "floating apex" nor a flash in the pan. They also must understand that nothing less than success will be acceptable, that they will be given the resources needed to succeed, and that their overall success in the organization will depend, in part, on their support for this program.

I'm not suggesting that you can motivate people by simply giving a speech or distributing a memorandum. It takes time and planning to build motivation. You can get early support by enlisting the aid of opinion leaders within the systems organization, but you and they must engage the support of all the data processing staff. It shouldn't be hard. After all, a successful internal control program has significant advantages for the data processing people: fewer late night emergency calls because the system is suddenly discovered to be out of balance, and a less traumatic annual external audit visit. Motivating staff is a long-term project, and demands constant attention to insure that DP people continue to be motivated.

A second factor critical to success is *providing the necessary training.* The underlying concept is very simple: You should not expect people to successfully carry out tasks for which they haven't been given proper training. It should be no surprise that many new products (like software packages) and techniques (like internal control) require skills that are not present in the target population (the data processing staff and the users). Obviously, if they had the skills relating to internal control, they would have used them, and the state of internal control in application systems would not be so dismal!

At the beginning, there doesn't have to be extensive training of everyone on the staff; you can start with a limited number of people. Begin by holding a meeting to explain the internal control classification tool, and distribute copies of the decision tree from Chapter 4. You could select several people to become "internal control gurus" and give them more extensive training.

The third factor is *integrating internal control into your systems development life cycle.* I'm amazed that managers can insist that their staff members do various things (like improve internal control) without making these actions a recognized part of their official systems development techniques. This makes no sense, since project managers are typically measured on the degree of compliance with the official life cycle. So if internal control is to be considered during the analysis, design, and implementation phases of systems development, the life cycle documentation must be modified to reflect that. The time required and the documentation for internal controls must be provided.

Fourth, *provide for walkthroughs and other controls over the process of building controls.* In introducing new techniques, we often fail to provide ways to insure that people are doing what is desired. A feedback program to inform you that people are (or aren't) doing what you need them to do is the key factor that separates programs that work from those that don't. If feedback tells you that things aren't going well, you can take corrective or remedial action. Without such a feedback program, your project to bring in new techniques can get into fatal trouble before you know that anything is wrong. Asking employees generally isn't enough. ("Are you putting good controls into your systems?" "Sure I am!")

In Chapter 8, I suggested that the walkthrough process is an effective way to monitor the internal control process. At first, you may want to establish additional controls. For example, you might assign a quality assurance specialist to work with the project teams to get the internal control program under way. (When quality assurance or internal audit assistance is unavailable, or when using it is politically unwise, limited consulting assistance might be used in its place.)

11.2.2 Building controls into new systems

Once a specific systems development project is selected for pilot testing your program of increased control awareness, you can develop a plan. This plan should provide sufficient pre-training for both the members of the pilot project team and key users on the concepts of this plan and internal control. Be certain to allow time in the pilot project's schedule to use the control tools and to permit walkthroughs. Provide a means for evaluating the success of the control awareness program. You should judge the quality of controls in the completed system and encourage feedback from pilot project participants. (Did they like or dislike the tools and techniques? Can they offer suggestions to improve the control awareness program?)

To be honest, I wouldn't drive people crazy about internal controls. What you are seeking, as I've said all along, is control consciousness. The biggest success with regard to internal control is simply getting your systems development staff to *think about controls*. That consciousness can move you in the right direction faster than any involuntary program. How can you achieve that consciousness in your own organization? First, let it be known that internal control is important, and that this is a long-term issue. Second, let it be known that people will be evaluated at least partly on their support of internal control. These are the keys to success!

11.2.3 Building controls into existing systems during maintenance

Another issue that frequently comes up is this: It's all well and good to build internal controls into new systems, but what about controls in existing systems? Isn't it important that they be well controlled too? Of course it is, but realistically, you aren't going to pull significant numbers of people off new development projects to retrofit controls into old systems. (It may not be possible even if you wanted to because some systems are built in such a way as to render them effectively uncontrollable.) However, there are some things that can be done when systems are subject to maintenance.

Specifically, a two-step process can be applied: First, determine whether the system is an asset control system, and thus requires control. Find out what controls have evolved in the user areas. (You will generally find that when there is an objective need for controls, the users will have evolved a manual control mechanism.)

Having done this, determine, perhaps using the decision tree, the form of control that would be reasonable to insert and that could be made during maintenance of a particular part of the system. I have often found that a few simple controls inserted into the system during maintenance can significantly reduce the user's manual control burdens.

I'm not suggesting that you rip apart every existing asset control system to build in controls. Only where you were going to perform maintenance anyway or where intervention can specifically be justified should control maintenance be performed.

11.3 Some final thoughts

In summary, I'd like to leave you with several thoughts.

Always keep in mind the value of the data you're dealing with. The information entrusted to our information systems is often vital to the survival of the firm. Our accounting and payroll records are irreplaceable. As I've pointed out, in more and more cases, there is no alternative but to use automated systems to process the volumes of data involved in today's operations in many industries. The value of that data and its potential effect on the survival of the organization represent a good justification for improving internal controls.

Unlike many other issues in data processing, top management understands the need for controls. Because members of top management often don't understand the details of data processing, they often take requests for new hardware or software at least in part on faith, or on the basis of faith in their data processing management. By contrast, internal control — auditability — is something they understand perfectly well. When the need for added control is explained, top management is usually very supportive of the control enhancement plans.

The threat of an audit is the poorest excuse for building good controls. For years, managers have tried to force systems developers to build well-controlled systems by raising the specter of the annual audit. They have turned the auditor into the bogeyman, someone to be feared. The true reason to build controls into systems is, of course, that controls are needed by *all* asset control systems.

Internal control is never achieved without a cost. In terms of time spent in either considering controls or having walkthroughs or both, there's some cost associated with the development of internal controls.

Careful planning is needed for a comprehensive program of internal control enhancement. As I said earlier, the degree of success in improving the state of internal control in application systems is directly related to the care taken in developing plans. The investment in planning will be repaid many times over. Without planning, though, chances of success will be extremely limited.

Always think control. The objective is control consciousness. If the systems developers and users are conscious of the need for control, most of the battle is won. The more natural the consideration of control becomes, the better the controls will be, and the more that control will be integrated into systems. It is a goal well worth pursuing.

Finally, thanks! In reading this book, you've indicated your interest in internal control in systems. Unfortunately, today that interest is rare. I hope that you find the concepts and tools presented here to be of use, and I wish you every success in developing and implementing your program to improve internal control in your organization.

Good luck!

Index

Acquisition review, 18, 30

Analysis phase, 4, 5, 16, 31, 71
  decision tree and, 55-69
  documentation, 112-22
  modeling controls in, 78-91, 112-14
  phase-related control and, 70-77
  review points in, 44-45
  walkthrough, 45

Analysis-time controls, 71-73, 78-91, 99
  current system and, 80, 85-86, 94-98
  review of, 115-16
  sources of, 79-81
  user policy and, 78-84, 90

Application controls: *see* Controls.

Application development review, 16, 30-31

Application systems control review, 15, 19-20, 30-31

Auditing:
  around the computer, 14, 17
  reviews, 15-20, 30-31
  structured techniques and, 4-5, 21, 28-31

systems development life cycle and, 16, 33-49, 75-77
  through the computer, 14

Auditing specialists, 18-24
  computer security, 22-23, 54
  external, 18-20
  internal, 20-21
  perception of, 24-28, 75-77
  quality control, 21-22, 48
  risk managers, 23-24
  tasks of, 15-20

Automated controls, 59-60, 65, 72-74, 84, 104, 106, 115, 117
  documentation of, 115, 117

Balance sheet audit, 15, 18-19

Batch control, 62-63, 86

Brooks, F.P., Jr., 129

Carry-forward notes, 72-74, 90-91, 99

Computer security: *see* Security.

Conservative development, 34-42

Control plan, 22, 138-44

Controls, 50-69
  analysis-time, 71-73, 78-91, 99
  automated, 59-60, 65, 72-74, 84, 104, 106, 115, 117

operations controls and, 104
quality assurance and, 106-109
user documentation, 105-106
Information systems auditing
management review, 18, 30
Input controls, 56-65
authorization test, 58-60
data conversion, 59, 61-64
error correction and resubmission, 56-59, 65
file maintenance input, 56, 57
inquiry input, 56, 57
internal process movement, 59, 64
transaction input, 56-65
verification test, 60-62, 64, 66-68
Insurance (risk management) specialist, 23-24

Logicalization process, 87-88, 121

Maintenance, 114, 126-37
debugging in, 129-31
review, 17, 30, 31, 135-36
syndromes and, 132, 133, 135
Manual controls, 11, 59-60, 65, 72-74, 84, 104, 106
documentation of, 115, 117-18
Metzger, P., 129
Minispecification example, 86
Model:
analysis controls, 78-91, 112-14
design controls, 92-101
logical, 87-88, 114, 116, 121
of current system, 80, 85-86, 94-98, 116
of rejects, 81-84
of run-to-run controls, 92-101
of sample audit trail report, 79
of user policy, 78-84, 94

physical, 88-89, 114, 116, 120

Operational system documentation review, 114-15
Operations controls, 104
Output controls:
control totals, 63, 68-69, 94
distribution totals, 69
verification controls, 60-62, 64, 66-68

Packaging process, 92-101
Page-Jones, M., 127
Phase-related control, 31, 70-77
analysis-time controls, 71-73, 78-91, 99
decision tree and, 71
design-time controls, 92-102
implementation controls, 71, 74, 103-10
Physicalization process, 88-89
Processing controls, 66-68
file and operator, 67
limit and reasonableness, 67-68
run-to-run, 64, 66-67, 71, 92-101, 104

Quality assurance, 90
specialist, 21-22, 48
systems testing, 109-10, 130
tools, 67
walkthrough, 45-48, 106-109

Radical development, 34-49
auditing and, 43-48
Rejects, modeling, 81-84
Reviews, auditing, 15-20, 27
acquisition, 18, 30
application development, 16, 30, 31

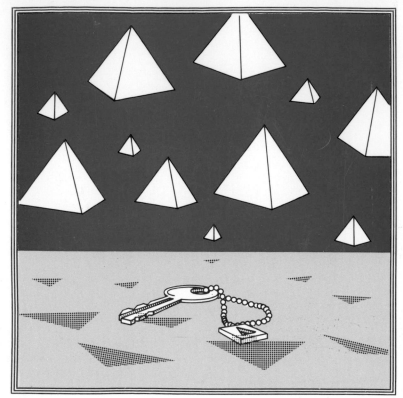

ABOUT THE BOOK

All systems need internal accounting controls to ensure the accuracy, completeness, and security of the system's data. In *Building Controls into Structured Systems,* Alan E. Brill shows how to identify the proper controls for your system and how to build and document internal controls as part of the formal systems development process. The book introduces the notion of *phase-related control* (PRC), a divide-and-conquer philosophy based on the concepts of the structured techniques. PRC is the process of specifying and documenting the internal controls appropriate to each systems development life cycle stage.

To guide you as a developer or an auditor in this task, Brill provides a tool based on a decision tree that can be used to identify controls in an existing system as well as in a system under development — whether you use the structured techniques or not.

ABOUT THE AUTHOR

Alan E. Brill is a Senior Consultant for Yourdon, inc. He teaches and consults in the areas of EDP auditing, internal control, and information security. Previously employed in the Management Consulting Services Division of the accounting firm of Ernst & Whinney, the author holds an MBA in systems management. He is a CDP and a Certified Information Systems Auditor.

CA 17
1126-46   ISBN: 0-917072-27-8
yourdon press 1133 avenue of the americas new york, n.y. 10036